D0520274

# FREEDOM'S FRAME

### RICK GREEN

***Freedom's Frame***

For additional copies of this book or for more information on other books, contact:

Revolutionary Strategies
P.O. Box 900
Dripping Springs, TX 78620
(512) 858-0974
www.rickgreen.com

Cover design:
Ashley Franks

Printed in the United States of America
ISBN   9780976935445

# DEDICATION

## Trey, Reagan, Kamryn, & Rhett

*The joy you have each brought to my
life is greater than I ever imagined
would be possible this side of Heaven.*

*I am driven by the desire to pass an intact
Torch of Freedom to each of you. I pray
you inherit the same passion to pass it on
to the next generation of Americans.*

## Graduates of Patriot Academy

*You are the modern day men and women of
Issachar…you understand the times and you
know what to do. Now go do it.*

# CONTENTS

# FRAMEWORK #4: "Consent of the Governed"

## Actions We Can All Take

# FOREWORD

There is something unusually gratifying about watching a young man grow and mature into a man of depth and moral strength and integrity. I have been privileged to meet and come to know Rick Green over the past twelve years, and I am delighted to be able to write this foreword for *Freedom's Frame*.

I don't recall when I've been more excited about a new book. Rick Green has done a masterful job of condensing a critically important message into a relatively brief book. Drawing on a vast resource of good ol' common sense, he here presents a very frank and honest revelation of his personal awareness of America's great need for Christians who will take their God-given responsibilities seriously, who are willing to be accountable to the Lord and to other Christians for their actions and behaviors.

I find in Rick Green a rare breed (unfortunately) of committed Christian political leader, one whose principles and philosophy other evangelicals can emulate without hesitation because they are biblical and scripturally solid.

*Freedom's Frame* beautifully sets out a clear explanation and refutation of today's popular concept of "the separation of church and state." Rick's understanding and explanation of America's remarkable free market/free enterprise system is exceptionally comprehensible, and he shares with his readers his interesting insights into the Founding Fathers' opinions and feelings toward slavery. He's done his homework – providing sources of his information as well as references and documentation to support what he writes.

I believe this is a book for today's America. It comprises both an alarming warning to those of us who care about our country's future, as well as a Clarion Call to move us to action. It is truly in the hands of every individual to stand up for and to propagate the freedoms established and supported by these United States of America.

Zig Ziglar

# ACKNOWLEDGMENTS

Let me make it clear right from the beginning, that most of the ideas put forth in this book are neither new nor purely original. My purpose is not to create a new frame or picture of our American freedom, but rather to dust off the current one. My goal is to magnify the time-tested principles that have formed the framework of our great nation and preserved the beautiful picture of American freedom that we have enjoyed for over two centuries. And, since I owe a great deal of my understanding of America's greatness to others, what I share in these pages is much to their credit.

I have been incredibly blessed to learn at the feet of exceptional men such as David Barton, Zig Ziglar, Dr. Charles Jarvis, Paul Tsika, Richard Halbgewachs, and my own father, Richard Green. I have spent a lot of time studying the lives of many of our nation's intellectual giants and powerful leaders such as President Ronald Reagan, Newt Gingrich, Dr. Kenneth McFarland, Ambassador Alan Keyes, Dr. Martin Luther King Jr., Milton and Rose Friedman, and many others. The writings and speeches of those who have gone before me have not only influenced my thoughts and positions but have inspired the writing of this book. Although a repackaging of many of the same principles and ideals that others have articulated in the past, my hope is that this book will help keep America's torch of freedom burning brightly in this generation, and be a light to the next.

Special thanks to Noreen Hay who turned my jumbled thoughts into something that makes a little sense.

Thanks to Ashley Franks for her amazing design work on this book and our DVDs.

To Bruce Upham, your friendship has truly sharpened my counsel. Thank you for holding me accountable to meet deadlines and push on to completion.

To David Barton, you live more like Christ than any other man I have ever known. Thank you for your example, your mentorship, and your friendship. Like many others, I am taking a leisurely stroll down a path that you labored long and hard to blaze. Generations are indebted to you for the role you have played in preserving our nation's heritage.

To Dr. Mac, how can I express thanks to a man who has been such a big influence on my life though we have never met. Although you are now in glory, your words live on. They have inspired me from childhood, (as I listened to your speeches in my father's car) and to this day, as I hear your wisdom being shared through friends such as Dr. Charles and Maxine Jarvis. Thank you Dr. Mac for being a midnight rider, I am indebted to your legacy.

Thanks to everyone on the *WallBuilders* staff, for all that you do behind the scenes to make it possible for this organization to have the tremendous impact that it does.

To the Torch of Freedom Foundation Board and supporters, thanks for investing in the next generation.

To Mom and Dad, thank you both for living out this book my entire life and instilling these principles in all your children and grandchildren.

To my wife Kara, thank you for pushing me to complete this project, and for finding time in our crazy schedules to get the work done. God truly has given me a wife who perfectly completes me. Of all the wonderful earthly gifts that He has blessed me with, you are by far the greatest.

And, most of all to Jesus, my Sovereign Lord, and Savior, thank You for the blessings of life, liberty, and the pursuit of happiness. I am truly grateful that though the duty to act is ours, the burden of results rests completely upon Your ever-capable shoulders.

# INTRODUCTION

*O beautiful for spacious skies,*
*For amber waves of grain,*
*For purple mountain majesties*
*Above the fruited plain!*
*America! America!*
*God shed His grace on thee,*
*And crown thy good with brotherhood*
*From sea to shining sea!*

**—America the Beautiful**
*Katharine Lee Bates*

The words of this song are right...America IS beautiful. My family and I have had the privilege of visiting almost every one of the United Sates and most of her famous landmarks, including Pike's Peak where Katharine Bates was inspired to write the poem that has become one of the most popular patriotic songs of all time.

But America is more than beautiful. She is also powerful, benevolent, and successful beyond all measure. She is more free and full of opportunity than any other nation in history. America has been a refuge, a hope, and a beacon of light to the rest of the world. Those who have sought to escape the bonds of oppression have made their way to her shores - she is the land of the free.

America's heritage is indeed, a rich, remarkable, and breathtaking tapestry, but unless each generation continues to build upon the same foundation that our Founding Fathers gave to us in the framework of our freedom, the American portrait will wither and fade.

Freedom such as we are blessed with in our country does not just happen by accident. The rights and privileges of self-government were purchased at a high price. Many lives have been sacrificed for the cause of American liberty, and throughout every generation, Americans have the responsibility to guard with vigilance the essential principles that hold our freedom firmly in place. Those essential principles consist of the four main elements, which I call *Freedom's Frame*, and that frame is in our hands today.

If the frame is discarded, the beautiful portrait of our American way of life will be lost with it. That is why it is important for us to realize that the future hope of freedom for our families, our churches, our workplaces, and our communities, depends upon how we handle *Freedom's Frame* today.

By preserving the framework that formed the foundation of America's success and has kept our individual rights and privileges intact thus far, we have a hope of duplicating the process in our generation and passing the torch of freedom onto our sons and daughters. Therefore, the goal in these pages is to layout a blueprint for preserving America's heritage by identifying the essential principles that make up the four-sided frame of our nation's freedom.

We're going to journey back to the late 1700's and early 1800's to discover the key elements that led to the extraordinary success of our nation. Obviously, one book cannot possibly cover all of the specific strategies that have grown out of what our Founding Fathers established. So, in choosing what to focus upon in this book the approach I have taken is a macro rather than micro one. I will be addressing the overriding principles (the frame around the picture) and not so much the intricate details of the portrait itself.

The four sides of *Freedom's Frame* that we will be examining in these pages are the very foundation of our American way of life. They are the basic ideals which have preserved our freedom for over two centuries and define us as a nation. Sadly, they are the same principles we are most in danger of losing today in the culture war that is raging within our society. However, it is not too late for us to change the tide and preserve the liberty we have inherited. We can ensure that the freedom we enjoy is passed on intact to our children and grandchildren.

My goal in this book is to help ordinary citizens who care about preserving American freedom for future generations, know what they can do today to make a difference. Therefore, some issues will not be covered in depth even though they are under attack. For example, the Supreme Court and its attempt to elevate itself above the Executive and Legislative branches of our government, directly affects our rights as citizens. However, the Legislative and Executive branches are the ones who need to reign in the courts. Although some of you may be current or future Members of Congress and able to do more in fighting those battles, our purpose here is to focus on what "we, the people" can do today to help preserve the basic framework of our American freedom and pass it on to future generations.

The four sides of *Freedom's Frame* that hold the picture of our American freedom and prosperity in place are elements found within our nation's birth certificate, the Declaration of Independence. We will explore each of these principles in this book:

1. *Self-evident Truths* (the undeniable fact that moral absolutes exist).

2. *Endowed By Our Creator* (our unalienable right to individual freedom)

3. *The Pursuit of Happiness* (the importance of free enterprise to our freedom).

4. *Consent of the Governed* (we each have a voice).

*We hold these **truths to be self-evident:** that all men are created equal, that they are **endowed by their Creator** with certain unalienable rights, that among these are life, liberty, and the **pursuit of happiness;** that to secure these rights, governments are instituted among men, deriving their just powers from the **consent of the governed**...*[1]

## *We hold these truths to be self-evident*

*Freedom's Frame* is built unequivocally upon moral absolutes. Our Founding Fathers began with the basic recognition that truth exists and is *"self-evident"* at that! No wishy-washy, as long as it "feels good" and does not "offend" anyone preconditions existed when the principles upon which our government were first established. Truth was the cornerstone that set the plumb line for our nation's strength. However, moral relativism is running rampant in America today and is totally out of line with that foundation.

## *Endowed by our Creator with certain unalienable rights*

The Declaration of Independence makes it crystal clear that our freedoms come from God, not government. Our rights as individuals do not come from commissioners, state representatives, governors, or any elected or appointed official. No matter how many ways judges may try to twist the intent of the

Declaration, it will never say that our rights come from a Supreme Court justice.

God is not only *in* the equation of our freedom - He is the center of it. Communism is incompatible with faith because it asserts that all rights and freedoms come from the government and not from God. The Founding Fathers of our nation believed the exact opposite. They believed we were each endowed by our Creator with certain unalienable rights.

## *Among these are life, liberty, and the pursuit of happiness*

The unalienable rights to life, liberty, and the pursuit of happiness meant very specific things to our Founding Fathers. In the Declaration of Independence, they described precisely what a violation of these rights looked like in the form of King George's actions.

Today, we see worse violations than these perpetrated by our own government, partly through our elected representatives but mostly through unelected bureaucrats. Thomas Jefferson wrote,

*A wise and frugal government, which shall leave men free to regulate their own pursuits of industry and improvement, and shall not take from the mouth of labor bread it has earned - this is the sum of good government.*[2]

# *Deriving their just powers from the consent of the governed*

The final side of the frame calls for every generation of Americans to do their duty in upholding our national freedom. The just powers of government can only come from the consent of those being governed: that means you and me.

The word "consent" is used three times in the Declaration of Independence and eleven times in the Constitution. It is a strong reminder that government's use of power without the consent of those governed, either individually or through their representatives, is tyranny. The problem today is that our silence is often mistaken as our consent. If we choose to be uninvolved in the process, those in power assume we consent to what is being done. The system we have been given works. It allows us to grant power to those in government, but the system will only work if we work the system. We do this with our voices, our pens, our votes, and our actions.

The formula for the continued success of our nation is not complicated; however preservation of *Freedom's Frame* will require our vigilance and action. The questions being asked of our generation today are simple:

*Will America's picture of freedom fade away prematurely, on our watch? Or will America be strengthened and reinforced, nursed back to full health, and made ready for the next generation?*

It is our duty as Americans to realize, reclaim, and restore the revolutionary strategies implemented by our Founding Fathers. If we keep them alive, Lord willing, freedom will survive for our posterity, and the portrait of their American way of life will be as breathtaking as ours has been.

# FRAMEWORK #1
## We Hold These Truths

*No people will tamely surrender their Liberties, nor can any be easily subdued, when knowledge is diffused and Virtue is preserved. On the Contrary, when People are universally ignorant, and debauched in their Manners, they will sink under their own weight without the Aid of foreign Invaders.*

**—Samuel Adams**
*From a letter to James Warren*
*Dated November 4, 1775*

# 1

# MODERN-DAY MIDNIGHT RIDERS

Many speakers and authors (like myself) travel around America today warning others of the dangerous trend that has developed in our culture. You might say we are the modern version of Paul Revere as we sound the alarm of an approaching enemy, in every corner.

Well, perhaps that analogy is a bit of a stretch, but the connection was forever formed in my mind during a recent visit to Boston, Massachusetts. I had an opportunity to walk along The Freedom Trail and visit Paul Revere's final resting place. I also saw the Old North Church where the lanterns were hung to let the riders know if the British were coming by land or by sea, and what came to my mind as I walked that historic trail were the words of one of the greatest orators of my lifetime, Dr. Kenneth McFarland. He had once made the point that the "riders" of today have a much more difficult job in some respects than the Midnight Riders did. It was easier for Revere to identify and point out the enemy, since they were the only guys in town wearing red coats. Today, the enemy is not as easily distinguished. They usually look just like us. Lately, they have even begun to sound like us, using religious language to cloak their secular purposes.

Indeed, "the enemy" today often does not even see themselves as America's enemy. They do not realize that the policies and cultural changes they advocate will destroy our nation. The threat comes not only from many of our politicians but also from influential religious leaders, professors, entertainers, journalists, and a host of others, whose ideology is more lethal to the American experiment than any heavy artillery.

The trend that is sweeping our nation is also affecting our churches and threatens to undermine the foundation upon which America is built. This enemy, which is increasing in popularity, is the postmodern, humanistic mindset of moral relativism. With its anything goes and everything's okay mentality, it is taking hold and unraveling every aspect of our American society. Today, we are told that what may be wrong for you is not necessarily wrong for me because we each determine right and wrong with our own set of standards, hence we are all doing what is right in our own eyes. Sound familiar?

Unfortunately, operating out of a well-intentioned but misplaced desire not to offend anyone, combined with a warped view of freedom, many Americans now believe the suggestion that anything is actually right or wrong for everyone is overbearing, pig-headed, simple-minded, old-fashioned, and intolerant. If these people had written the Declaration of Independence, they would have never said, "*We hold these truths to be self-evident.*" They would have opted for language more acceptable to all and offensive to none. Something such as:

*We hold the following suggestions and ideas to be possible, as long as no one takes offense or objects, in which case we will find a more politically correct, non-offensive way to express what we think might be good ideas for a new nation.*

Really inspiring stuff, isn't it? It might be humorous if it were not so prevalent and dangerous to the freedom we enjoy in this nation.

## Caught in a Trap...

I recall debating an atheist professor a couple of years ago at Texas A&M University. He was a very kind gentleman, like most are who do not realize the damage their rhetoric is doing to this nation. He was not gruff, rude, or overbearing. In fact, he was exceptionally likeable and we had a respectful interaction, but regardless of how harmless the packaging, the theories this man advocated are more dangerous to this nation than enemy tanks or missiles.

The best question of the evening came from a student. She asked the professor, "Do you believe there are any moral absolutes?" His reply was "No." To which she said, "Are you absolutely sure?" Everyone, including the professor, knew exactly where she was going, but he had no way to avoid the obvious trap. He replied, "I am." She had her victory and replied, "So the only absolute is that there are no absolutes; sounds like a shaky theory to me."

It is more than a shaky theory: it is quicksand for all who embrace its philosophy. It is also the most dangerous weapon formed against the safety and freedom of mankind. One does not have to be a philosophy major or a student of history to realize where moral relativism will lead. Such thinking is exactly what led to the Nazi scourge.

Like a dangerous disease, which seems unthreatening at the start but turns deadly over time, the danger of this philosophy begins slowly - in the name of fairness, equality, and tolerance - but before long it will lead to increasing government restrictions upon the rights and freedoms of individuals. Without a solid, unchangeable standard of right and wrong that is passed from one generation to the next, our nation's freedom and safety will depend upon whether those in power at any given time are benevolent or tyrannical.

Of course, we know from Jeremiah 17:9 that the heart of man is *"deceitful above all things, and desperately wicked."* Man tends towards corruption, this truth our Founders knew, and it is the reason why they created a government that consisted of three separate branches.

The Separation of Powers does not allow absolute power to reside in the hand of any one person or branch.[3]

## Building on a Rock...

However, our government goes farther than establishing a system of checks and balances. With an immovable set of truths that govern our nation, we have a system of law that is established on immovable principles. That is why if we remove the Bible, which is the basis of our laws, we will no longer have a bedrock foundation, and anything will go.

The opposite is also true. Good government cannot exist without moral absolutes. They are the foundation that will ensure anything will NOT go. They are also the reason why the American experiment resulted in peace and prosperity for over 230 years, rather than conquering and destruction. When the basis is kept intact, the frame is strong, and America is a positive influence upon the entire world.

The moral relativist is appalled by what you just read. They see the concept of "American Exceptionalism" as arrogant because they do not believe one set of values is any better than another. I remember the first time I came across this type of attitude. One of these tie-dye-wearing, tree-hugging, "every set of values is equal" characters came up to me after a speech and said, *"American, so what? Big deal! What is so special about being an American?"*

Okay, so maybe he wasn't wearing a tie-dye shirt or hugging a tree right then, but his comments made me imagine he went straight home to do both! I was not sure how to respond to such nonsense. Just as Barbara Mandrel was country before country was cool, my family raised me to be patriotic before it was cool.

One positive outcome of the attack on America on September 11, 2001 has been a rekindling of the camaraderie and esprit de corps of our people as a whole. An instant renewal of patriotism swept our land as people began waving Old Glory and standing together, no longer as hyphenated Americans, but simply as Americans. The renewed patriotism in our country is a significant occurrence we have needed for quite some time. However, our success in fighting the War on Terror has lulled people into believing the winds of catastrophe have died down. As the shock of 9/11 begins to fade into history, we must move from a renewed patriotism to an *informed* one.

When we wave the American flag, we must teach our children why that particular flag is worthy of being waved and what it represents. We must remind ourselves that America is different than other nations. We have responded to the events of history differently than any other, and we have become the banner of freedom and prosperity for the world.

Despite this unprecedented record of national success, moral relativists are completely apathetic about our heritage and often antagonistic to anyone patriotic.

## Some Fool Has Stolen Your Letterhead....

As a Christian conservative in the political arena, I have gotten more than my fair share of hate mail from those types. As a member of the Texas Legislature, I had a very simple form letter drafted in response to such hateful correspondence. The letter simply read:

*Dear Sir/Ma'am,*

*Apparently, some fool has stolen your letterhead, is writing ridiculous letters on it, and signing your name. I just thought you would want to know about it. Have a nice day.*

Well, that might help you understand why I am no longer serving in the Texas Legislature! Seriously, I borrowed that letter from one of my friends and mentors, Dr. Charles Jarvis, but my staff would never let me mail one of those responses out.

So, how exactly DO we respond to someone who hates our country or says *"America...so what?"* The best answer I've ever heard was from Ambassador Alan Keyes. He said he responds to those types by asking them a simple question. He asks them, *"Why do you think we call the last century, 'The Great American Century'?"* And then proceeds to give them the answer:

- America led the way in saving the world not once, not twice, but three times from the evils of Nazism, communism, and despotism.

- Americans are the only people in the history of the world to hold a technological advantage in war and not use it for conquest.

- America could have controlled the entire planet in 1945 with the atomic bomb. Instead, the weapon was used to liberate people around the world. No nation in history has ever done that.

- America spent her own dollars to rebuild the countries that waged war against her.

Why do we respond so differently? Why does America not take advantage of opportunities to conquer the world? Because the value system upon which our nation is built is unique - it is revolutionary. Because the framework of our government recognizes certain self-evident truths, it prevents us from taking away the rights and freedoms of others. In fact, it actually compels us to export freedom around the world as best we can.

Think of what the world would look like if America had been established without these moral absolutes. To help your imagination a little, think of what would have been the outcome if the atomic bomb had been in the hands of someone with the power, control, and morals of Hitler, instead of in our hands. The millions of lost lives, during World War 2, would have been multiplied by tens of thousands.

So, as nice and politically correct as it may sound, all value systems are NOT equal: truth matters a great deal. I make no apology for the truths upon which America has been built, and even though we have made our share of mistakes as a nation, I am proud of our overall record. Because the framework of our government recognizes and is guided by certain "self-evident truths," we have gone out of our way to right our own wrongs and to extend freedom to those beyond our borders.

While the framework designed by the Founding Fathers may be seen as revolutionary to our modern world, it remains essential to our continued success. The concept of moral absolutes must be reinforced in our culture.

# 2

# CAREFUL NOW...THE KIDS MIGHT SEE THAT!

Today, moral relativists are working hard to prevent absolute truth from being taught. If their efforts succeed in removing God and/or any reference of biblical truth from our society, they will destroy not only the framework of our freedom, but also the rich portrait of our American way of life.

The Ten Commandments, which form the basis for our civil and criminal systems of law, are no longer permitted to be on display in our public schools today. In *Stone v. Graham,* the Supreme Court declared a Kentucky law requiring that the Ten Commandments be posted in public schools as being unconstitutional. The Court said,

> *If the posted copies of the Ten Commandments are to have any effect at all, it will be to induce the schoolchildren to read, meditate upon, perhaps to venerate and obey the Ten Commandments.*[4]

Oh my! Now there is a dangerous activity for our children that must be stopped! Allowing children to read the Ten Commandments is not permissible as a state objective under the Establishment Clause because children might obey them!

How long do we need to think about the nonsense of that court's ruling? What will it take before we realize the detrimental effect it will have upon society when we can't tell students not to kill or steal for fear they may start obeying?

To see the direction our country is heading, all you need to do is ask yourself what the two major changes to public education have been in the last fifty years.

1. Moral absolutes have been removed from our value system. No standards exist any longer. Every student decides on their own what is right and what is wrong. The lesson these students are being taught is that they can do whatever is right in their own eyes.

2. We teach our children that they and their classmates are not created by God, but instead are randomly gathered protoplasm - an accidental pile of atoms. This has put a new formula in place and removed God from the equation. We should not be surprised when that results in a devaluing of human life.

Consider the astronomical increase in violent crime within our schools in recent years. Columbine, Jonesboro, Paducah, Pearl, Virginia Tech, and unfortunately the list keeps growing. In America fifty years ago, it was unheard of for a student to walk into a classroom, take out a gun, and murder his or her classmates, but in February 2008 alone, we had four school shootings.

Even if people do not have the same exact belief system or religious affiliation, anyone with common sense should recognize that society is better when the majority recognize a Supreme Being. The child across the table is not randomly gathered protoplasm; he is a child created in the likeness of God, and if I commit a crime against him or her, I am doing so against a creation of God.

Unfortunately, this concept is slowly being eroded from our culture. The massive increase in violent crime would not have surprised our Founding Fathers. As Benjamin Rush, signer of the Declaration of Independence and father of our public schools under the Constitution, warned:

> *In contemplating the political institutions of the United States, I lament that we waste so much time and money in punishing crimes, and take so little pains to prevent them. We profess to be Republicans and yet we neglect the only means of establishing and perpetuating our republican forms of government; that is, the universal education of our youth in the principles of Christianity by means of the Bible.*[5]

Today we have attorneys from the American Civil Liberties Union (ACLU) running around the nation opposing any mention of God or recognition of moral absolutes in the public square. They are even opposing the use of the founding document, which made their freedom possible. Yes, they have actually opposed the teaching of the Declaration of Independence because of the references to truth and to God contained in it.

But upon what grounds are such objections based? How can they oppose the Declaration of Independence? What threat are they protecting us from? What great harm are they trying to prevent from happening?

Answer. All they need is one person who says they were offended by an expression or felt left out because they do not believe in the same truth expressed in public by others, and that's enough. If one person dissents, they will fight to limit the rights of everyone else.

## Prayer Before a Football Game

*Santa Fe v. Doe* was the case that prohibited prayer before a football game for precisely that reason.[6] The school district did not require students to pray during the welcoming time before the game. However, they allowed the students to decide how they wanted to welcome the people at the beginning of each game. The students elected a fellow student before the game, but could not impose an activity upon that student. The elected student was free to choose his or her own way of welcoming people to the game that day. The elected student decided to say a prayer as simple as, "God, protect the guys out on the field, so that nobody will get hurt tonight." The Supreme Court said a prayer as simple as this was unconstitutional, essentially because someone in the stands might be offended.

In an effort to avoid the offense of one, the court is now prohibiting the free exercise of faith by everyone else. Newsflash to the court: The Declaration of Independence does not say, "Life, Liberty, and never be Offended." It says, "Life, Liberty, and the pursuit of Happiness."[7]

But the court's ruling removes the rights of every citizen because one person, who had the freedom not to participate, was offended. This is exactly the kind of government interference the Founders intended to prevent, but when freedom's frame is removed, the principles used to make decisions are based on whatever the currently elected officials or appointed judges feel they should be. These kind of ridiculous rulings are the inevitable outcome.

We start to restrict one group out of "fairness" or "tolerance" to another in order to prevent anyone from being "offended." Note to the ACLU and the courts: now I'm offended, and so are millions of other Americans. Why is it that they work so hard to keep the one from being offended, while caring nothing about the 999 that will be offended by the removal of God from the public square?

## The Pledge of Allegiance...Unconstitutional?

Courts are now restricting more than religious expression. They are stretching the boundaries of moral relativism to even advocate for a neutral approach to basic American principles. For instance, in *Newdow v. U.S. Congress*, the Ninth Circuit Court of Appeals had a problem with more than just the phrase "under God" when they ruled the Pledge of Allegiance was unconstitutional. From an important paragraph in that decision, we see their objection went deeper. It says,

> *To recite the Pledge . . . is to swear allegiance to the values for which the flag stands, unity, indivisibility, liberty, justice, and . . . monotheism. Recitation of the Pledge aims to inculcate in students a respect for the ideals set forth in the Pledge. . . and thus amounts to state endorsement of those ideals.*[8]

Think about what the court has said. They said not only do they have a problem with "under God," they believe it is unconstitutional for the state to inculcate in the minds of young people such bedrock American principles as: liberty, justice, and indivisibility. The court does not want the state instilling these values because it means taking a stand, declaring certain principles as good and true, and therefore rejecting moral relativism. Yet, the teaching of such bedrock principles is necessary to the preservation of freedom.

It is ironic that the entire court opinion mentioned only one phrase from our founding documents: the first part of the First Amendment. The rest of the discussion is about the decisions of the Ninth Circuit and the Supreme Court over the last forty years. In other words, a few ivory-tower elite "geniuses" are pontificating about what other "geniuses" said, not what our Founding Fathers have said or what the Constitution says.

This snowball effect can only be reversed one way. By introducing once again, the original intent of our Founding Fathers, and requiring actual changes to the Constitution through the amendment process. This process allows all Americans to be involved rather than just a handful of unelected judges who are trying to refashion our freedoms to suit their personal opinions.

It is in this realm of jurisprudence that the clash between moral absolutes and moral relativism exists. Those who advocate moral absolutes are "originalists." They believe in bedrock principles, and want the Constitution to stand as it is, unless the people agree to amend it as allowed under the provisions of Article V.[9]

The moral relativism crowd wants the Constitution to be a "living, breathing" document. Sound good, but what it means is that they want it to change with the wind, be moved by whatever is popular, and by the political opinions of whoever happens to be sitting on the Supreme Court. This approach to freedom, rights, government power, and the law leads to complete erosion of individual liberty because there are no standards by which to be held accountable. In this environment, NONE of our freedoms are secure, which was the very reason for giving government power in the first place, according to the Declaration of Independence.[10]

## Who Owns the Land?

However, this is not just about religious liberty; it is about every American liberty. Once the foundation is gone and self-evident truths and unalienable rights are no longer a guarantee; all our freedoms are up for grabs.

A perfect example is the egregious *Kelo[11]* decision handed down by the Supreme Court a couple of years ago. The intent of the framers was made clear through the Constitutional prohibition on eminent domain. It allows the government to take ownership of private land only for public use such as roads. Yet, the Supreme Court in all its wisdom decided to destroy this principle of our freedom established over 230 years ago. In *Kelo*, the court allowed a local government to seize private property and sell it to another private entity for development simply because the local government wanted a higher tax base on the property.

Think of the ramifications. Now local governments can target tax-exempt churches that own property in prime real estate locations. Greedy bureaucrats and local officials would like to see the increased revenue that would come if that prime land were transferred to a builder who would use it to build shopping malls or the like.

I am certainly not against shopping malls or progress. And I firmly believe in the free market and allowing people to do what they want with their land. Our founders considered this as the "pursuit of happiness," which literally means the freedom to own your own property and pursue your interests in the market.

However, the result of *Kelo* is really just the opposite. It means that a person or group can lose the ownership of their property if the government does not want them to own it anymore. It is probably one of the worst Supreme Court decisions of the last fifty years, and that is saying a lot considering how bad some of them have been. In this decision, the principles established by the Founders were disregarded and the concept of "unalienable rights" was thrown out the window. If truth or justice depends on the whims of whoever is in power, then American liberty is lost.

This erosion of property rights is also happening at the hands of local officials. Cities and counties use the power of government to enforce "development standards," which dictate to private landowners what they can and cannot do with their own land. Even in some instances, requiring them to set aside a portion of their property for "green space." If people want green space, they should contribute to organizations that buy up land for that purpose. Philanthropy groups, such as Ducks Unlimited, a group I support, preserves wetlands through raising private funds.

Rather than using their own funds, self-righteous environment worshippers use the power of government to trump individual ownership rights in lieu of group rights. They take private property from someone who worked hard and purchased it, then give it to the public, often without compensation.

When truth is relative, so is freedom. When the fact that we are "endowed by our Creator" with certain rights is recognized by all, then we each have equal protection. When God is removed from the equation of freedom, no true freedom can exist.

It is time to recognize the need to reestablish moral absolutes and allow truth to regain its rightful place in the fabric of our nation. If we desire to preserve the freedoms we enjoy and the continued success of our nation, this strategy of our Founding Fathers must again be a part of our national consciousness.

Fundamental to this process is simply acknowledging the existence of God and the fact that He is the source of our freedom. It is impossible to have truth and moral absolutes without having God in the equation. *With* Him, everything else makes sense.

That brings us to the second side of *Freedom's Frame*, "Endowed by our Creator."

# FRAMEWORK #2
## *Endowed by our Creator*

*I . . . recommend a general and public return of praise and thanksgiving to Him from whose goodness these blessings descend. The most effectual means of securing the continuance of our civil and religious liberties, is always to remember with reverence and gratitude the source from which they flow.* [12]

**—JOHN JAY**
*First Chief Justice of the*
*U. S. Supreme Court*
*1789-1795*

# 3

# THE TRUE SOURCE OF AMERICA'S STRENGTH

When terrorists attacked our nation on September 11th, 2001, their plan was to hit us at the core of our strength. A hatred for freedom and the American way of life set them on a course of destruction. They aimed their aggression at what they believed symbolized the framework of our society - American free enterprise and military might - and they took their best shot. However, the cowards who committed these acts of war actually missed the mark.

Even though they inflicted a terrible wound, they did not cause us to crumble as they had hoped. In fact, their actions had the opposite effect. Instead of crippling us, Americans were roused to a new level of national unity. The terrorists were unsuccessful because they misunderstood the true source of America's strength.

America's strength is not found in our skyscrapers and architectural structures, though they are monuments to the ingenuity and entrepreneurship of our people. America's strength is not found in our wealth and materialistic belongings, though they are a testimony to the success of our capitalistic system. America's strength is not found in our military installations - even the Pentagon itself - though they stand as bastions of freedom and fortresses of great power.

The true source of America's strength is imbedded deep within our legacy as a nation. What began over 230 years ago as an experiment in individual freedom and personal liberty has become the framework of the most powerful and successful nation on earth today. Preserving these ideals that framed our country's social, political, and economic landscape is the only way to ensure that our children will inherit the same freedoms we have enjoyed.

The strength of America today is a by-product of the passion, goodness, and foresight that guided our Founding Fathers in establishing our unique system of rule - a government *of the people, by the people,* and *for the people.* A Government that recognizes and honors the God-given rights and freedoms of all its citizens, while limiting the amount of power and control it exercises over them.

In the aftermath of 9/11, the enemies of the United States discovered that America's goodness should never be confused with weakness. By cowardly attacking civilians of our nation, they attempted to extinguish the torch of American freedom. But that flame will never be quenched by such overt and cowardly acts. What was clearly intended for evil, inflamed the passions, patriotism, and righteousness that lay within the soul of this great nation.

However, the greatest threat to the future of our country does not come from those who would attack us from without, but rather from those who attack from within. If Americans forget that the source of our nation's strength comes from our faith in God, then America will cease to be a great nation. Our frame, which has held the beautiful portrait of freedom in place all these years, will break apart.

These words (attributed to the 19th century French philosopher, Alexis de Tocqueville[13]) say it best:

*I sought for the key to the greatness and genius of America in her harbors and her ample rivers...; in her fertile fields and boundless forests...; in her rich mines and vast world commerce...; in her public school system and institutions of learning. I sought for it in her democratic Congress and in her matchless Constitution. Not until I went into the churches of America and heard her pulpits flame with righteousness did I understand the secret of her genius and power. America is great because America is good, and if America ever ceases to be good, America will cease to be great.*

## The Secret Ingredient

The fundamental source of America's strength and the secret to her success is the philosophical, spiritual, and political understanding that America was founded as a nation *under God*. The framers of our independence recognized that faith in the Divine Providence of God was essential to good government. That is why faith was, and still is, an integral part of the framework that governs this nation.

Because America was founded on godly principles, we have become a refuge for the rest of the world. In every generation, those longing for a better life for themselves and their children have come to America to find it. Our arms are open because we believe that each person has certain unalienable rights, given to him by his Maker, which are not to be restricted by any form of human government.

Yet, America has not always upheld its own high standard. Some dark clouds hang over our nation's history. Other than the holocaust of abortion, the darkest cloud of all is that of slavery. Indeed, this blight is still felt among our people today. So, it begs the obvious question: If our Founding Fathers were men of faith, if they believed in a biblical worldview and set out to establish a nation under God, then how could they have allowed such a shameful abomination to continue unchecked?

Many, if not most, of those involved in the founding of our nation were anti-slavery. Even though some had inherited slaves themselves, they abhorred the whole system and worked to eradicate it. Although they did not put an end to slavery in 1776, what they did do was set in motion the very principles and tools that would lead to its rightful destruction some eighty-five years later. It was upon the principles cited in the Declaration of Independence that Abraham Lincoln based the Emancipation Proclamation, in 1863. For a more thorough discussion on this subject, please see Appendix C: *Slavery and the Founding Fathers by David Barton.*

What our Founding Fathers gave us was an ideal which they envisioned over time would become more of a reality. Indeed, their experiment in self-government has led to the expansion of rights and liberties for all Americans. In 1776, they risked their lives to secure the God-given rights of future generations, and today that same foundation remains as the true source of America's strength.

# 4

# A GODLESS CONSTITUTION?

The media today often portrays our Founding Fathers as atheists, agnostics, and deists. Modern textbooks such as *The Godless Constitution* teach these falsehoods on college campuses and law schools around the country.[14] This reflects a growing mindset, which seeks to entirely eradicate God, and specifically Christianity, from the public square. It is typical of a philosophy that is gradually being introduced into the education of America's youth. While it may not be affecting you personally today, those who are being indoctrinated with these errors will eventually have an effect on us all.

Whatever is being taught in the classroom today, will undoubtedly show up in government tomorrow. Those being taught a godless worldview will vote for leaders who reflect the same beliefs. Indeed, some may even be candidates themselves, taking their godless opinions directly from the classroom into our legislatures and courts.

The Herculean effort being made to remove even the mention of God from every corner of American life not only completely ignores the facts about the founding of our country and the intent of the framers of our independence, but also fosters blindness and a growing ignorance among the American people. This trend will give way to increasing incidents of bad judicial decisions and legislation that will chip away at our personal rights and erode our freedoms.

## Graduation and God

We have already begun to see the effects of this philosophy unfolding in our courtrooms. For instance, in *Commonwealth v. Chambers*,[15] a man was sentenced to death for robbing a seventy-year-old woman of her social security check and beating her to death with an ax handle. The sentence was appealed, and though the court acknowledged that it was a horrible crime, they vacated the death sentence simply because the prosecutor had mentioned a Bible verse in the courtroom.

We already looked at *Santa Fe v. Doe,* where in the small town of Santa Fe, Texas, the court held that there could be no prayer before a football game.[16] In a previous case from the same small town, *Doe v. Santa Fe Independent School District*[17], the question of student-led prayer at a graduation ceremony was addressed. The federal court decided in its ruling that they would only allow a "typical, non-denominational prayer" to be said. Graduation prayers could refer to God or the Almighty, but could not refer to Jesus. The court warned that a

United States Marshal would attend the graduation. If any student mentioned Jesus in a prayer, that student would be summarily arrested and face up to six months incarceration - just for mentioning the name of Christ at a public school graduation.

In the state of Nevada, on June 15, 2006, a Las Vegas high school student, Brittany McComb, mentioned how her personal faith in Christ had contributed to her academic success. As she spoke at her own high school graduation ceremony, the public school officials reacted by shutting off the microphone in the middle of her speech in order to avoid such offensive language from being uttered.[18]

Recently, a guest on our radio program, *WallBuilders Live! with David Barton and Rick Green*, told us a true story that had my blood boiling. Our guest that day was Mat Staver. Mat is the founder of Liberty Counsel and the Dean of Liberty University School of Law. He told us that one of his clients, Erica Corder, was involved in a dispute with her Colorado public school. They had refused to release her diploma unless she signed a public apology for mentioning the name of Jesus Christ as part of her valedictorian address.[19]

I can only imagine the reaction those who founded this nation would have to such court rulings. John Adams, one of our Founding Fathers and the second President of the United States, said that our nation was established upon the general principles of

Christianity.[20] Yet, today, 195 years after his statement, our citizens are being penalized by court rulings, which say that if Americans mention the name of Christ in a public forum, we should be arrested and put in jail.

This is a monumental cultural shift, which has enormous repercussions for the future of this nation. This shift has occurred primarily over the last forty years. The reason for this sudden change is that we no longer know our history; we do not know the foundation upon which our nation was established. When court decisions prohibiting the mentioning of Jesus in public prayer occur, instead of being outraged and demanding our rights as Americans, too many think, *"Oh well, the judges know more about the law than we do, so what they say must be right."*

One simple question that does not get asked often enough is this: If our Founding Fathers did not want prayer in schools or Christ's name mentioned at graduations, etc., why didn't they remove those things themselves?

When the Ninth Circuit Court of Appeals ruled that the Pledge of Allegiance was unconstitutional,[21] many in our nation finally woke up. Those who have been actively involved in these debates used to joke that one day a court would declare that Americans could not recite the Pledge of Allegiance any longer, and we would have to remove the words "In God We Trust" from our currency. We used to laugh at the idea because it was totally absurd, but the day we heard the decision from the Ninth Circuit Court, we stopped laughing.

## Following a Bad Example

You may be surprised to hear me say this, but from a modern day purely jurisprudent point of view, the Ninth Circuit Court got it right. Their ruling was not right from a Constitutional or historical point of view and certainly it was not right from a principled point of view. However, all the Ninth Circuit Court did that day was follow what the Supreme Court has been doing for the last forty years - they simply took the next logical step along the same crooked path.

The Supreme Court has systematically set out to remove God from the framework of our nation, and the Ninth Circuit Court just went one step further. The real questions Americans need to ask are: Has the Supreme Court been getting it right for the last forty years? Is the godless path they have steadily been going down the right direction for our nation? Has it expanded our freedoms?

Woodrow Wilson was once quoted as saying,

*A nation that does not remember what it was yesterday, does not know what it is today, nor what it is trying to do.* [22]

This is where America is right now. We do not know where we came from, or what we are trying to do as a nation any longer. In the last forty years, we have lost our identity, and as a result we now find our foundation has shifted. We are no longer one nation under God.

# 5

# ATHEIST FOUNDING FATHERS?

With all the misinformation about the faith of our Founding Fathers that is being touted as truth today, is it possible to know what these men actually did believe? Does any proof exist to refute all the lies? Or can anybody say anything they want today about what these men thought and how they lived, and go unchallenged?

I'm so glad you asked!

Should one want to know if a Founding Father was a man of faith, it is not hard to find the answer. All they need to do is a little investigative work.

What our Founders believed about God is easily discerned by reading the journals, books, and written correspondence of these men and those who knew them best. It would be the same if someone wanted to find out about you two hundred years from now. They would read your private journals (or maybe your emails!) and what others who knew you said about you, and they would quickly be able to ascertain what you believed and how you lived.

So, the problem is not lack of proof: the problem is that people simply do not ask. They believe what the "experts" say and do none of the legwork themselves.

In this book, I will share some of what I have discovered about the strong faith of our Founding Fathers from my own studies into the lives of these men. This is not an exhaustive work, although one great resource you may want to pick up if you are interested in digging a little deeper is David Barton's book, *Original Intent.* My hope in the next few pages is to simply expose the false idea that these men were atheists, agnostics, and deists by looking at a few of their lives and what we know to be true about them.

## GEORGE WASHINGTON

Charles Thomson, secretary of the Continental Congress, and General Henry Knox, both wrote of times when they came to see George Washington and found him in prayer.

Many paintings exist depicting George Washington and other Founding Fathers in prayer. One particular painting is based on the account of Isaac Potts, an account that was also recorded in Reverend Nathaniel Randolph Snowden's diary:

*I was riding with him (Mr. Potts) in Montgomery County, Pennsylvania near to the Valley Forge, where the army lay during the war of ye [sic] Revolution. Mr. Potts was a Senator in our State and a Whig. I told him I was agreeably surprised to find him a friend to his country as the Quakers were mostly Tories. He said, 'It was so, I was a rank Tory once, for I never believed that America could proceed against Great Britain whose fleets and armies covered the land and ocean, but something very extraordinary converted me to the Good Faith!'*

*'What was that,' I inquired?*

*'Do you see that woods, and that plain?' (It was about a quarter of a mile off from the place we were riding.)*

*'There,' said he, 'laid the army of Washington. It was a most distressing time, and all were for giving up the Ship but that great and good man [Washington]. In that woods I heard a plaintive sound, as of a man at prayer. I tied my horse to a sapling and went quietly into the woods and to my astonishment, I saw the great George Washington on his knees alone, with his sword on one side and his cocked hat on the other. He was at Prayer to the God of the Armies, beseeching to interpose with his Divine aid, as it was ye [sic] Crisis, and the cause of the country, of humanity and of the world. Such a prayer I never heard from the lips of man. I left him*

*alone praying. I went home and told my wife. I saw a sight and heard today what I never saw or heard before, and just related to her what I had seen and heard and observed. We never thought a man could be a soldier and a Christian, but if there is one in the world, it is Washington. She also was astonished. We thought it was the cause of God, and America could prevail.'*

*He then to me put out his right hand and said 'I turned right about and became a Whig.'*[23]

Isaac Potts switched parties (from Tory to Whig) after witnessing George Washington in prayer.

At Valley Forge, the large monument to Washington depicts him in prayer, as does the stained glass window in the chapel. In the United States Congress, a stained glass window in the private prayer room also depicts our nation's first President in prayer.

Is it not amazing to you that a supposed atheist or deist was willing to pray so often and so powerfully that it would cause someone who witnessed his secret petitions to be so moved by them that he would switch political support!

## GOUVERNEUR MORRIS

Gouverneur Morris was a signer of the Constitution and a very influential Founding Father. He spoke more than any other man during the Constitutional Convention and penned the words to the Constitution. He took the concepts discussed at the Constitutional Convention and put them into writing.

Fifty years ago, a mention of him was in every one of our textbooks. Children learned his name and knew about his contribution to our freedom. Today, he has virtually disappeared from our educational system. Why? Because some of the statements he made during his lifetime are now deemed politically incorrect. For instance, he said:

*Religion is the only solid basis for good morals, therefore education should teach the precepts of religion and the duties of man toward God.*[24]

Think about that for a moment. What he was saying is that education and religion ought to work together; i.e., the role of education is to teach the duty of man toward God. Yet, today, our courts tell us the exact opposite. They remove any mention of God from the educational system and claim they are doing so because of the Constitution - the very document that Gouverneur Morris penned with his own hand. I think it is safe to say that Morris, more than any other man who ever lived, understood what the Constitution meant and what it was intended to do. Yet, because of revisionist history, Morris is now considered politically incorrect, has been erased from the textbooks, and is no longer an influence in the lives of Americans.

# JAMES WILSON

James Wilson was another one of our distinguished Founding Fathers. He was one of George Washington's original appointees to the Supreme Court and wrote commentaries on the Constitution. He was a signer of the Constitution and the second most active member of the Constitutional Convention. He also signed the Declaration of Independence. It is difficult to identify a better eyewitness to the birth of our nation or a better expert on the law than him. However, James Wilson is no longer a name that is taught to our children. His contribution to the founding of our nation is no longer valued because, according to modern standards, some of the statements he made are also deemed politically incorrect. For instance, he said,

*Human law must rest its authority ultimately upon the authority of that law which is divine. . . . Far from being rivals or enemies, religion and law are twin sisters, friends, and mutual assistants. Indeed, these two sciences run into each other.*[25]

Here he draws a descriptive word picture of how religion and law are natural allies. Wilson believed that man's laws must rest upon the ultimate authority of God's law.

# WILLIAM SAMUEL JOHNSON

William Samuel Johnson was another signer of the Constitution. He is one of my personal favorites because he loved doing something that I also love to do. He loved to speak at graduations and encourage young people to appreciate their freedom and make the most of what they have been given.

However, Johnson would be unable to participate in graduation ceremonies in our public schools today in the same way he did in his day, because of a case called *Lee v. Wiesman.*[26]

*Lee v. Wiesman* dealt with prayer at public school graduations and was decided seven years before the *Doe v. Santa Fe* case we looked at previously. The prayer in this case was a prayer that was given by a clergyman rather than a student. The school had asked Rabbi Gutterman to pray at the graduation, but gave the instruction that it was to be a "secular prayer" since the graduation was a "secular event."

The liberal Unitarian Universalists may be able to pray secular prayers, but I doubt the instructions made much sense to the Rabbi. He apparently decided that what the school wanted must be a politically correct, non-offensive prayer. So, he prayed such a bland prayer that during the trial the lawyers argued whether the Rabbi actually even prayed that day! It was not offensive to anyone, but the problem was created because the

Rabbi mentioned "God" at the beginning of the prayer. The court said the use of "God" was psychological coercion and unconstitutional at a public school graduation.

Indeed, if our court's modern interpretation of the Constitution agrees with the original intent of the men who wrote it, then how do we explain the following words of Constitution signer William Samuel Johnson, given at a public school graduation?

*You . . . have received a public education, the purpose whereof hath been to qualify you the better to serve your Creator and your country . . . Your first great duties, you are sensible, are those you owe to Heaven, to your Creator and Redeemer. Let these be ever present to your minds, and exemplified in your lives and your conduct.*[27]

Referencing the Bible, from Acts 17:28, he proceeded to tell the students that it was in God that they lived, and moved, and had their being.[28] Johnson was preaching at a public school graduation! Today, this would be ruled unconstitutional under the very Constitution that he helped create and then signed.

## JOHN WITHERSPOON

The Reverend Dr. John Witherspoon was a pastor who signed the Declaration of Independence and served in Congress. As odd as this might sound to us today, it was common for clergymen to play a role in government at that time. Out of the fifty-six signers of the Declaration of Independence, twenty-nine held what we would today call seminary degrees. While liberal seminaries may churn out atheist ministers without the blink of an eye today, it would have been quite an accomplishment for "atheists" to get seminary degrees in the 1700's.

Witherspoon was responsible for two translations of the Bible and his sermons were so well known across the colonies you could call him the Billy Graham of that day. He also trained a number of the Founding Fathers at what is now Princeton University.

## A FEW OTHER *"ATHEIST"* EXAMPLES

Charles Thomson, Secretary of Congress, was responsible for the translation of the Thomson Bible.

Benjamin Rush started the Philadelphia Bible Society, the first Bible society in America.

Francis Hopkinson put together the first American hymnal by putting the Psalms to music.

Abraham Baldwin, founder of the University of Georgia, was offered a professorship of divinity at Yale when he was twenty-three years old. He also served as a chaplain during the Revolutionary War.

Charles Cotesworth Pinckney and John Langdon started the American Bible Society. This Bible Society spreads hundreds of millions of Bibles around the world every year.

James McHenry started the Baltimore Bible Society.

Jacob Broom, John Dickinson, and Roger Sherman wrote major treatises on the doctrines of Christianity.

These are just a few examples. We could, literally, go on for quite some time! The truth is, among those who built the framework of our nation were many of the greatest theologians of their day. Yet, our modern media portrays them all as atheists, agnostics, and deists. How do they get away with doing this?

Simple - by taking isolated statements from about a dozen of the 250 men who comprised the group known today as our Founding Fathers, (men such as Thomas Jefferson and Benjamin Franklin, whose political ideas were not fully in line with a biblical worldview) and deducing from just a few of those statements that all of the 250 Founding Fathers were atheists, agnostics, or deists. But even Thomas Jefferson would not be considered a deist in the sense that we understand the word today.

A true understanding of the faith of the men who framed our independence is hardly possible if we chose to ignore the contribution of those who lived active Christian lives. The truth is that ninety-five percent of the founders were men with strong religious convictions. They believed in Jesus and worked to ensure that the government they were forming reflected biblical truth. These facts are stubborn things, backed up by indisputable evidence, yet ignored by our modern historians.

# 6

# BUT WAIT...THERE'S MORE!

When one starts to uncover the faith of our Founding Fathers, it begins to feel like one of those late-night television infomercials where the voice over guy just keeps piling on more and more "stuff" until it just seems ridiculous to get so much for only $19.95.

Well, the evidence of the faith of our founders is so overwhelming that when I am giving a live presentation, I often have to stop for a minute and say, "But wait...there's more!"

So just in case you might be thinking the last chapter was a cherry-picking episode, let me offer a few more examples, and we will even include a man who was considered one of the LEAST religious of our Founding Fathers.

## FIRST MEETING OF THE U.S. CONGRESS

The United States Congress met for the first time on September 7, 1774, as recorded in the Annals of Congress. Congress opened with prayer. What is interesting about this prayer is that it lasted approximately three hours! Think about it. The first thing this so-called group of atheists, agnostics, and deists did was to spend not one, not two, but **three** hours in prayer!

Silas Deane wrote that it was a prayer worth riding one hundred miles to hear.[29] That is equivalent to driving fifteen hundred miles today, just to hear a prayer. Deane said it was so moving that even the stern Quakers had tears in their eyes.

John Adams recounted this event in a letter to his wife, Abigail:

> *When the Congress first met, Mr. Cushing made a Motion, that it should be opened with Prayer. . . . The Motion was seconded and passed in the affirmative. Mr. Randolph our President, waited on Mr. Duche, and received for answer that if his health would permit, he certainly would. Accordingly next morning he appeared with his clerk and in his pontificallibus, and read several prayers, in the established form; and then read the Collect for the seventh day of September, which was the thirty-fifth Psalm. You must remember this was the next Morning after we heard the horrible rumor, of the Cannonade of Boston. I never saw a greater effect upon an audience. It seemed as if Heaven had ordained that Psalm to be read on that morning. . .*
>
> *I must beg you to read that Psalm.[30]*

## BENJAMIN FRANKLIN

Benjamin Franklin is the man whom both sides of this debate agree was one of the least religious of our Founding Fathers. Franklin was eighty-one years old at the Constitutional Convention. Consider that age in the founding era for a moment. Eighty-one was an age I used to consider "old," but I no longer believe that. I had the privilege of speaking at a couple of events with Congressman Ralph Hall a few years ago. He had just turned eighty-one. When he took to the podium, he looked over at me and said, *"Rick, I used to think eighty-one was old. But when I attended Senator Strom Thurmond's 100th birthday party last year, he looked over at me and said 'Oh, to be eighty again!'"*

In the founding era, the average life span was thirty-five, so at eighty-one, Franklin was an elder statesman and well respected by his colleagues. When he spoke, people listened.

On June 28, 1787, he rose to give one of the most important speeches of the convention. If you read the journals, this was a moment of great contention where it looked as if all was lost, agreement could not be reached, and the delegates could possibly go home empty handed. Addressing his colleagues, Franklin began:

*In the beginning of the contest with Great Britain, when we were sensible to danger, we had daily prayer in this room for Divine protection...*

Now, before we go any further, these comments must be put in context. He is one of only six that signed both the Declaration of Independence and the Constitution. Those six were now at the Constitutional Convention, but eleven years previous they had signed the Declaration of Independence in the exact same room with all the odds against them, and they believed the only way the war would be won was if God was on their side. Divine Providence had to step in if they were to have any hope of victory. Franklin recalled how badly the odds were stacked against them then, and continued:

*Our prayers, Sir, were heard, and they were graciously answered. All of us who were engaged in the struggle must have observed frequent instances of a superintending Providence in our favor... [H]ave we now forgotten that powerful Friend? Or do we imagine we no longer need His assistance? I have lived, Sir, a long time, and the longer I live, the more convincing proofs I see of this truth—that God Governs in the affairs of men. And if a sparrow cannot fall to the ground without His notice, is it probable that an empire can rise without His aid?*

*We have been assured, Sir, in the Sacred Writing, that 'except the Lord build the House, they labor in vain that build it.' I firmly believe this; and I also believe that without His concurring aid we shall succeed in this political building no better than the builders of Babel…*

*I therefore beg leave to move—that henceforth prayers imploring the assistance of Heaven, and its blessing on our deliberations, be held in this Assembly every morning before we proceed to business…*[31]

As David Barton says, this least religious Founding Father sounds like a Bible thumping evangelical of today!

When the Supreme Court (or anybody else) says the Founding Fathers did not want public expressions of faith, we should remind them that even the least religious Founding Father implored the delegates at the Constitutional Convention to open each day with corporate prayer and to remember our great need for God's help.

## NOAH WEBSTER

Noah Webster was much more than just the author of the most famous dictionary in the world. He was a Founding Father, a soldier, an elected official, a writer, and a Christian. The memoirs of his life describe his personal commitment to Christ:

*...he took up the study of the Bible with painful solicitude. As he advanced, the objections which he had formerly entertained against the humbling doctrines of the Gospel were wholly removed. He felt their truth in his own experience. He felt that salvation must be wholly of grace. He felt constrained, as he afterward told a friend, to cast himself down before God, confess his sins, implore pardon through the merits of the Redeemer, and there to make his vows of entire obedience to the commands and to devotion to the service of his Maker.*[32]

However, the best evidence that someone lived out the faith they professed is the way they are thought of by their peers. How would you like to be remembered in the same way as Noah Webster? It was written of him: *Noah Webster taught millions to read, but not one to sin.*[33]

## JOHN QUINCY ADAMS

John Quincy Adams also lived an amazing life. He was a Founding Father and the son of another Founding Father, John Adams. At the age of eight, he was doing musket drills with the Massachusetts Minutemen. He served as Secretary of State, U.S. Senator, President of the United States, and then spent the last seventeen years of his life in the House of Representatives as the leader of the anti-slavery forces. He earned the name, "the Hell-Hound of Slavery" for his opposition, laying the foundation for its eventual abolition.

Despite his amazing resume and most assuredly busy schedule, he took time to study the Bible daily and made it a priority to instill in his son a love for reading the Scriptures. Adams wrote to his son:

*My Dear Son,*

*I have thought if in addition to the hour which I daily give to the reading of the Bible, I should also from time to time (and especially on the Sabbath) apply another hour occasionally to communicate to you the reflections that arise in my mind upon its perusal, it might not only tend to fix and promote my own attention to the excellent instructions of that sacred Book, but perhaps also assist your advancement in its knowledge and wisdom.[34]*

Doug Phillips, founder of Vision Forum, has compiled John Quincy Adams teachings into a book entitled, *"The Bible Lessons of John Quincy Adams for His Son."* It is an excellent teaching tool which can be found at www.visionforum.com.

The personal writings of many other Founders reflect equally succinct declarations about their faith in Christ. In closing, consider a few of these quotes, which were taken from a book by David Barton entitled, *Original Intent.*

*On the mercy of my Redeemer I rely for salvation and on his merits; not on the works I have done in obedience to his precepts.*[35]

**—Charles Carroll**
*Signer of the Declaration of Independence*

*For my part, I am free and ready enough to declare that I think the Christian religion is a Divine institution; and I pray to God that I may never forget the precepts of His religion or suffer the appearance of an inconsistency in my principles and practice.*[36]

**—James Iredell**
*U.S. Supreme Court Justice*

*I .. am endeavoring .. to attend to my own duty only as a Christian.. let us take care that our Christianity, though put to the test .. be not shaken, and that our love for things really good wax not cold.*[37]

**—William Samuel Johnson**
*Signer of the Constitution*

*May I always hear that you are following the guidance of that blessed Spirit that will lead you into all truth, leaning on that Almighty arm that has been extended to deliver you, trusting only in the only Saviour, and going on in your way to Him rejoicing.*[38]

**—Francis Scott Key**
*Attorney; Author of the "Star Spangled Banner"*

*I desire to bless and praise the name of God most high for appointing me my birth in a land of Gospel Light where the glorious tidings of a Saviour and of pardon and salvation through Him have been continually sounding in mine ears.*[39]

**—Robert Treat Paine**
*Signer of the Declaration of Independence*

*My only hope of salvation is in the infinite transcendent love of God manifested to the world by the death of his Son upon the Cross. Nothing but his blood will wash away my sins. I rely exclusively upon it. Come, Lord Jesus! Come quickly!*[40]

**—Benjamin Rush**
*Signer of the Declaration of Independence*

It would be easy to fill a whole book with page after page of evidence revealing both the public and personal faith of our Founding Fathers. However, my goal for this book is to provide some strong examples, hopefully more than just anecdotal evidence, proving that these were men who not only had a public show of faith but who also were deeply devoted followers of Christ in their private lives as well. I encourage you to read Chapter 6 in Original Intent, *The Religious Nature of the Founding Fathers,* for a more exhaustive list of the faith of the men whose lives helped frame our nation.[41]

If our Founding Fathers were given the opportunity to speak to us today, what do you think they would say? I believe they would implore us to keep God at the center of both our public and personal lives. The biblical worldview publicly professed and personally lived out by these men is the glue that holds the frame of our nation's freedom together.

# 7

# WHAT ABOUT SEPARATION OF CHURCH AND STATE?

*Almighty God, we acknowledge our dependence upon Thee, and we beg Thy blessings upon us, our parents, our teachers, and our Country.* [42]

These are the simple words of a voluntary prayer, which the Supreme Court ruled as being unconstitutional in 1962 and banned it from being recited by children in our public schools. The court based their actions entirely upon one phrase, "*separation of church and state.*"

Wherever I speak on college campuses, almost every student in the audience is familiar with that phrase. The words, "separation of church and state" have become the political mantra of this generation. However, those same students are seldom as familiar with quotes taken from the Declaration of Independence or the Constitution, and when I ask them to tell me in which document the phrase "separation of church and state" is found, invariably someone will respond, "It is in the Declaration of Independence."

When I answer, "No, you will not find it in the Declaration," someone else will respond, "It is in the Constitution."

An answer of, "No, it is not in the Constitution either," often sparks a heated debate (especially at law schools) with a chorus of objectors clamoring to remind me of the Constitutional Separation of Church and State found in the First Amendment.

To which I reply, "Are you sure it is found in the First Amendment? Let's look and see…"

*Congress shall make no law respecting an establishment of religion, or prohibiting the free exercise thereof. . . .*[43]

…anyone see the word "separation?" How about the words "church" or "state?"

Of course, someone will then say, "Well, that is not what it says, but that is what it means." Already convinced they can determine the intent of the statute, we begin a discussion on legislative intent.

## The Meaning of "is"

To understand the "intent" of the legislators who pass any law, one must look at the journal that recorded the discussions that took place at the time the law was being debated. Or one must read the writings of the legislators who passed the law. Doing so is akin to cracking open their heads and peering into their minds to find out what they were thinking and, therefore, what they were intending.

The system still works the same way today as it did in the beginning. A legislator will address the floor from the front of the room and explain the bill, stating the case for why it should become law. The debate then begins. Opponents will ask questions or challenge sections of the bill. Supporters will throw "softball questions" at the author to help bring out the full meaning of the bill. All of this discussion is then transcribed and included in the journal, which can then be read by any interested person.

Why do they do this? Because, if years after a law is passed, confusion arises about certain portions of its meaning, or questions are raised of its intent, the answers can be found in the Annals. Let's face it, sometimes the legal language that is found in pieces of legislation can be hard to decipher, even for our elected officials who have been trained in understanding these documents. At times, even Presidents can have difficulty with grasping the true meaning of the simplest of language, (such as the meaning of the word "is") and they may need some help in coming to a fuller comprehension of the intent and meaning of the law.

The journal allows us to go back and discover what the legislators were thinking on the day they were discussing the law. What did they envision as the intended and expected application? This information was deemed so necessary to our correct interpretation of intent that a provision in the Constitution requires that everything said on the floor of the House and Senate be recorded in a journal, for this very purpose.[44]

This means that we can go all the way back to the discussions held between our Founding Fathers and discover exactly what those Congressmen intended when they passed the laws that govern us today. All we need to do is simply open up the Annals of Congress.

If we go back and read those transcripts, we will find that considerable time was spent debating the First Amendment to the Constitution. From June 8th to September 25th 1789, Congress discussed the details and parameters of this amendment. Yet nowhere in the Annals of Congress or the writings of the Founding Fathers who drafted the First Amendment, will you find the phrase "separation of church and state."

## Original Intent of the First Amendment

Fisher Ames provided the wording for the First Amendment in the House of Representatives. He did not say anything about "separation of church and state" in his debate, nor may it be inferred as his intent. In fact, Fisher Ames said something that would be ruled unconstitutional because of the court's modern application of that very phrase, "separation of church and state." He said, *"Not only should the Bible be in our schools, it should be the primary textbook of our schools."[45]*

Earlier, at the time of the Constitutional Convention, the founders discussed the individual rights of American citizens, which would later become the Bill of Rights. How many times did they mention the phrase "separation of church and state?" Zero. They did not talk about it once.

The phrase "separation of church and state" was not even introduced into the American vernacular until a little over a decade after the First Amendment was adopted. The phrase is exactly that - a phrase. It is not a statute, it is not a law, and it is not an amendment to the Constitution. It is simply a phrase lifted from a letter written by one of our Founding Fathers, Thomas Jefferson.

Jefferson was writing to the Danbury Baptist Association on January 1, 1802, in response to a letter wherein they raised their concerns about religious liberty ever being infringed by the American government. Jefferson responded that this would not occur because the Constitution builds "a wall of separation between Church and State."[46] So much has been erroneously inferred from that one statement. (I encourage you to read David Barton's article in the November 2003 issue of the Notre Dame Law Review for a more thorough treatment of Jefferson's intent.)

Simply stated, Jefferson was using the phrase to describe the Free Exercise Clause of the First Amendment, which says, *"or prohibiting the free exercise thereof."* The protection of our rights to live out our faith without government interference is what was being expressed both in the letter and in the First Amendment.

The Supreme Court twisted the meaning of the First Amendment by isolating those eight words from this personal letter from Jefferson.[47] They did not even consider the letter in its full context.[48] Then, in 1962, the Court used the phrase to completely remove God from all governmental institutions.[49] It is amazing how the court can ignore history and rewrite it to fulfill their particular agenda and purpose.

## We've Got the Wrong Guy

Perhaps even worse than misapplying Jefferson's words is the fact that Jefferson's words were used in the first place as a means for discovering the intent of the First Amendment. Actually, Thomas Jefferson and his words "separation of church and state" are irrelevant when it comes to interpreting the intended meaning of the First Amendment because Jefferson did not give us the Constitution or the Bill of Rights.

When a biographer wrote to Thomas Jefferson, to congratulate him for his influence on the Constitution, his response was,

> *One passage of the paper you enclosed must be corrected. It is the following. 'I will say it was yourself more than any other individual that planned and established the Constitution.'* [50]

Jefferson pointed out to the biographer that he *"was in Europe when the Constitution was planned, and never saw it until after it had been established."* [51]

Nor was Thomas Jefferson one of the Congressmen that passed the Bill of Rights, which contains the First Amendment.

So, arguing what the framers' intent was by using Thomas Jefferson as an expert witness on the First Amendment is the same as having a murder trial where the judge allows those who were not at the scene of the murder to come forth and tell us what happened. It is intellectually dishonest and a piece of cleverly crafted creative history at best, to say that Thomas Jefferson's words provide the intent for the First Amendment. To understand the original intent of the First Amendment, you must scrutinize the thoughts of those who took part in the debate, the ones who actually gave us the First Amendment.

That debate emphasized the need to avoid another Church of England being established in

America. In other words, they were trying to prevent a national denomination from being forced upon the citizens. None of their comments reflected intent to separate religious principles from government or from the public square. Just the opposite: they wanted to foster free expression, not political oppression.

For those who still want to rely on Jefferson as their expert regarding the First Amendment, it should not go unnoticed that exactly two days after writing his letter to the Danbury Baptists, he attended the weekly church service being held at the U.S. Capitol. These were religious services that he had helped to start and faithfully attended throughout the remainder of his presidency.[52]

It appears that Jefferson's views were far removed from the interpretation of them by our modern courts today. Would Jefferson, a man who himself established and attended religious services while holding the office of the President, really think that it was against the good of our nation or our citizens for children to pray for their teachers, parents, and country at the beginning of each school day? You decide.

# 8

# THE PERSONAL EQUATION

It is easy to point our fingers at corrupt and immoral politicians and blame liberal judges and groups like the American Civil Liberties Union (ACLU) for pushing forward their godless agendas on our society. We can connect much of the unrighteousness that has taken root in our land today to many of their actions; they have had a negative effect on us all. However, as citizens, how quick are we to recognize our own responsibility for the road we have taken as a nation?

In Romans 1:21-22, Paul wrote:

*Although they knew God, they did not glorify Him as God, nor were thankful, but became futile in their thoughts, and their foolish hearts were darkened. Professing to be wise, they became fools.*

Notice he said, *"Although they knew God...."* As we attempt to evaluate the reasons why America has lost its moral compass, this becomes an important exhortation to Christians today. It is something we need to seriously, and personally, consider.

Our Founding Fathers provided a framework of freedom that was based firmly upon the Christian principles they held. As a result, these men marched a predominantly civilian army into battle against the most formidable world power of the day and won. As we saw previously, these men also portrayed godly leadership and citizenship in the way they conducted their public and personal lives. Their example of duty to God and country was strongly conveyed in all their actions. They knew their God and led their lives accordingly. This sense of personal responsibility to God and country is something that is missing in the Christian community today.

## The Buck Stops Here

I admit it is easier to blame our nation's moral decline on the liberal judges who usurp their power and deny public expressions of faith while permitting every other kind of speech and activity - no matter how perverse - as long as it is not Christian in nature. It is outrageous that at this time in our history, when children are murdering one another in school, anyone actually thinks that our most pressing problems stem from too much religious expression!

However, we cannot rant and rave and place the blame on others without recognizing the powerful influence God's people can be (and have been) in our nation. It is untrue to say that America's cultural shift is solely the result of the actions of our governing officials without acknowledging the culpability of Christians who have personally failed to lead the way.

Our nation's immoral leadership is largely the result of apathy on the part of our people. Christians are especially to blame for this. Paul wrote that those who knew God were no longer glorifying Him as God. They had become fools. By not keeping God at the center of our personal lives as believers, we have in essence surrendered to the enemy and opened a way for God to be removed from the center of our public life. Deuteronomy 8:11-14 warns against this destructive tendency among God's people toward forgetfulness:

> *Be careful that you do not forget the LORD your God, failing to observe his commands, his laws and his decrees that I am giving you this day. Otherwise, when you eat and are satisfied, when you build fine houses and settle down, and when your herds and flocks grow large and your silver and gold increase and all you have is multiplied, then your heart will become proud and you will forget the LORD your God.*[53]

Until we keep God at the center of our *personal* lives, America cannot possibly hope to experience Him at the center of our *national* life. In Romans 1:28, Paul continued:

*Even as they did not like to retain God in their knowledge, God gave them over to a debased mind, to do those things which are not fitting.*

I cannot help but see a correlation between this passage and America today. While the judges and the lawmakers bear their share of responsibility, so do individual believers and the Christian community, who as a whole have allowed apathy and ease to rule over us instead of God. We need to recognize that the seeds of our own destruction were planted long before any of the cases that have limited our religious expression were ever brought before the courts or any of the liberal officials were ever elected into office. Government policy has simply followed the lead of individual desires and we are, in effect, reaping our own harvest.

Is it possible to turn back the tide? Will we ever realize the American ideal of being *One Nation Under God* again?

## The #1 Battlefield

I do believe freedom's frame (though splintered) is still in place today. However, I have come to realize that if we have any hope of seeing the reality of what our Founding Fathers envisioned ever coming to pass, it will not be simply because we have built a strong political machine. You may be surprised to hear me express this, but our success is not going to come merely because we elect the next Ronald Reagan to come riding to our rescue on a white horse. Nor will it happen just because we register every Christian voter in America or gain the majority in Congress and every State Legislature across the nation. Realization of the highest hope for this nation will not be assured even if we win the right to pray once again in our public schools and forums.

All of these things are very important and worthy of our united time, effort, and attention, but they are the fruit of something far more essential that is needed in order to assure America's freedom remains alive and intact for future generations.

Only when we realize that the cause of freedom is served more powerfully by what happens in our homes and houses of worship than what is happening in the White House or State Houses across our land, will we be on the right course once again. When citizens acknowledge that our individual rights, freedoms, and liberties come from God, and begin exercising them in the light of His authority over us, then we will begin to see the tide turning.

I guess what I am saying is that what we are doing on the political front is really quite insignificant when compared to what we are doing on the home front. Many of us were rightly upset about the Supreme Court's decision to prevent our children from having a time of student-initiated prayer before a Friday night football game, but how many of us have parent-led prayer in our own homes before the kids ever leave the house?

What do you think is more important, a ceremonial prayer at a football game or true communion with the Creator in our own homes?

What good is the freedom of religion in public arenas, if we are not exercising that same freedom in our private devotions?

We can pass all the righteous laws we want, but what do they mean if they are not a living reality in our businesses, backyards, and neighborhoods?

What those nine Supreme Court Justices do in Washington for or against the cause of freedom is not nearly as important as what you and I are doing in our own homes and communities to make those principles a living reality of American life.

Please understand what I am saying. I have devoted my professional career to being a freedom fighter and waging the political battles necessary to preserve our freedom to worship and maintain a public, national acknowledgement of God. I firmly believe that we all have a DUTY to do that today. But what does it really matter if we preserve a national show of freedom, if we are not really living freely? It is nothing more than hypocrisy to become enraged in the public arena regarding prayer at a football game, if I am not praying with my children in my own home.

I became convicted about my own efforts to live out the freedoms we have been given, after one court decision that consumed an enormous amount of my time and energy. I realized that if I had spent as much effort fighting the spiritual battle, as I had the political one, I would have been far more victorious. I recognized that God has given us so much in America. It is not that we are more deserving than our brothers and sisters who are living under despotic rulers or communistic regimes - it is actually despite our depraved sin nature that He continues to bless us.

Yet, with all these benefits of liberty, fellowship, and brotherhood that we enjoy in this nation, we are all too often guilty of spending more time grooming our hair or deciding what we are going to have for breakfast, than we are in acknowledging the One from whom our blessings flow. Being thankful for God's gift of freedom to us and giving praise to Him as our Savior and rightful Ruler over our nation, is the true and lasting source of America's strength.

## Training for Battle

A few years ago, a friend of mine who serves actively in the United States Army, spoke to the congregation at our church. On that morning, he shared with us the amount of time he and his men spend, each day, training for a battle that, hopefully, will never take place. He talked about the hours of preparation needed to ensure they would be ready to face an enemy attack. He then compared his rigorous physical routine to our spiritual lives. Unlike the military drills, which may never lead to conflict on the battlefield, our daily spiritual disciplines are what keep us victorious in the ongoing warfare that is taking place every day of our lives. That spiritual battle involves everyone and everything that we hold most precious - our spouses, children, families, friends, churches, communities, and even our nation.

We get incensed when we learn of the things being promoted in public schools these days; everything from evolution to homosexuality to free condoms for our teens, and idolatry in the form of worshipping the environment, etc. Yet, with what weapons are we fighting this battle?

If the world has your children for eight hours during the day, what are you doing in the evening to guarantee the right foundation is being laid in their hearts and minds.

The image this soldier gave was a powerful reminder of the reality of our lives as Christians. He helped me to realize my responsibility to fight the spiritual battle with the same intensity with which I fight the political ones. I began to see that every time I was too tired to read the Bible with my children or talk to them about God in the evening, I was choosing the political battle of the day over my children's spiritual battle of tomorrow. Nothing that any of us do in the course of our lives is more important than what we are doing in our own spiritual lives and in the spiritual lives of our families.

Our elected officials are important, yes, but they are not the key to God's principles being lived out in American homes today. You are the key to that happening! So, pick up the weapons God has given you and recommit to fighting the good fight of faith by acknowledging your God and living according to His principles.

# 9

# A NEW GENERATION IS GETTING IT RIGHT

Some say, *"But look at how tough it is. Look at all the corruption around us: the media, the entertainment industry, the textbooks. How much worse can it get?"*

Well, to be frank, it could be a lot worse! Let's not forget that in Noah's day, he was the only righteous one left, and when Elijah thought he was the only one left, God said, "No, there are 7,000 who have not bowed down to Baal."

Regardless of all the bad news that we read in the newspapers and hear on the evening news, despite the hostility of the Supreme Court towards religious freedom, despite the embarrassment of corruption in the political and business world, we stand among millions of others in this nation who refuse to bow to Baal. Literally, the good news is that millions of American citizens are still seeking God and His will to be done in their lives, despite their own weaknesses and failures. America is still the most blessed nation on earth today, regardless of our problems, and we still have a large, strong remnant of patriot believers who are willing to serve God and fight the good fight for the cause of American freedom.

Remember what God told Joshua when it was time to take Jericho? He said:

*Have I not commanded you? Be strong and of good courage; do not be afraid, nor be dismayed, for the LORD your God is with you wherever you go.*[54]

Regardless of who is elected to political office, we too have the Highest Official on our side.

## There is Hope

The reason I am optimistic about the future of America and have faith that our values will not be lost in the next generation, is because of what I have seen in audiences across the nation. I have the privilege of teaching at youth programs and have met a new generation of great Americans who are being raised up right now. I have talked to their parents, who have chosen to devote time and energy to lay a strong Christian foundation in their sons and daughters, despite what the world around them is doing. They are making a much more important investment in the future of their family and our nation, than anyone on Wall Street. Instilling godly values and a biblical worldview in a child today will mold them into men and women of integrity tomorrow.

"Families First" is a slogan some political parties put on banners and in their literature. But for many of the families I have met those words are a living reality.

Regardless of what the politicians are doing and saying, these families have made the choice to live their lives for the Lord and to raise their families to a higher standard - God's standard. As a result, this is a generation of young Americans who know the Lord and understand who they are and what they are doing.

If we want to have another "Great American Century," then we must return to those same truths upon which our nation was built. Yes, we should demand that our legislature require the teaching of these truths in our public schools, but more importantly, we should instill them in our own families and exercise them in our homes.

During the Continental Congress, Benjamin Rush sat next to John Adams and asked him if he thought we would succeed in our struggle with Great Britain. Adams did not answer with a great military or political strategy. He simply said, *"Yes, if we fear God and repent of our sins."*[55]

The Founders understood what mattered most. They knew that to assure victory over the enemy and success as an independent nation they needed to recognize that no matter how eloquent their speeches, how righteous their cause, how well drafted their documents, or how hard fought their battles; it all paled in comparison to their relationship before God. As we attempt to live out the strategies they implemented both nationally and personally, we need to remember that the only way we can do so is by keeping God at the center of all our plans.

# FRAMEWORK #3
## The Pursuit of Happiness

*Each individual of the society has a right to be protected by it in the enjoyment of his life, liberty, and property, according to standing laws. He is obliged, consequently, to contribute his share to the expense of this protection; and to give his personal service, or an equivalent, when necessary. But no part of the property of any individual can, with justice, be taken from him, or applied to public uses, without his own consent, or that of the representative body of the people.*

**—John Adams**
*Thoughts on Government*
*1776*

# 10

# THE INVISIBLE HAND

"Life, liberty, and the pursuit of happiness" are words from the Declaration of Independence that we all know. However, the "Pursuit of Happiness" meant something specific to the Founding Fathers of our nation that is not fully conveyed in our modern vernacular. The words were based on the writings of one of the greatest philosophers of the seventeenth century, John Locke, whose well-known phrase "life, liberty, and the pursuit of property" was later adopted by our First Continental Congress. What was in view by the founders as the unalienable right of every human being was the belief that government does not have the authority to hinder the economic ability and freedom of its citizens to build a good and prosperous life for themselves.

This truth is one of the fundamental pillars of the American way of life, and it is the third side of the frame that holds the picture of American freedom firmly in place. Benjamin Franklin said a free market is *"...the means, under God, of recovering and establishing the freedom of our country entire, and of handing it down complete to posterity."*[56]

Our Founders believed America's freedom depends upon the principles of free enterprise being exercised and preserved from one generation to the next. This belief was based on an understanding that allowing individuals to pursue what was in their own best interests, without the interference of government, was the best way to insure that the interests of the nation as a whole would be served.

Thomas Jefferson's draft of the Declaration of Independence replaced the word "property" with the word "happiness." However, he did not make this change on a whim. Jefferson refined the phrase based upon Locke's own writings, specifically the following passage from *An Essay Concerning Human Understanding*, (under a sub-section entitled, *The necessity of pursuing true happiness, the foundation of all liberty*):

*As therefore the highest perfection of intellectual nature lies in a careful and constant pursuit of true and solid happiness, so the care of ourselves, that we mistake not imaginary for real happiness, is the necessary foundation of our liberty. The stronger ties we have to an unalterable pursuit of happiness in general, which is our greatest good, and which, as such, our desires always follow, the more are we free from any necessary determination of our will, to any particular action, and from a necessary compliance with our desire set upon any particular and then appearing preferable good, till we have duly examined whether it has a tendency to or be inconsistent with our real happiness: and therefore till we are as much informed upon this inquiry as the weight of the matter and the nature of the case demands, we are, by the necessity of preferring and pursuing true happiness as our greatest good, obliged to suspend the satisfaction of our desire in particular cases.*[57]

What Locke, Franklin, and Jefferson all believed was that given the right to make decisions in an open and free market, our individual choices will not only serve our own personal interests, but benefit everyone else as well. Therefore, the guarantee to the "pursuit of happiness" is more than a quest for temporary fleeting pleasure. It is the acknowledgement of the inherent right within us all to cast a vision for our lives and sustain a course in that direction.

Adam Smith, an economist with perhaps the greatest influence on the American system, called this concept the "*invisible hand.*" What he meant by that was within a free market system each individual's decision to do what is best for his own interests will always have an unseen effect on others. More to the point, the personal pursuit of happiness will positively impact society as a whole. He wrote:

*It is not from the benevolence of the butcher, the brewer or the baker, that we expect our dinner, but from their regard to their own self interest. We address ourselves, not to their humanity but to their self-love, and never talk to them of our own necessities but of their advantages.*[58]

*Framework #3: The Pursuit of Happiness* has as its foundation the belief that the collective result of the individual decisions that Americans make each day does more to promote the interests of the nation as a whole than an individual bureaucratic decision made on behalf of the collective populace ever could. To give a practical example of how this philosophy works itself out in the marketplace, let's look at one specific industry - cell phones.

When 250 million American cell phone users decide for themselves the features that they desire and the services that best suit their evolving needs, it results in a growing industry that is constantly producing products that offer consumers far more and better options. The same benefits could have never been attained if a governmentally controlled agency set the standard for all users.

Simply stated, a free market system will always define the best products and set the best prices.

# 11

# FREE MARKETS VERSUS REGULATED MARKETS

While staying with our example of the cell phone industry, let's turn our attention now to the benefits of free markets over regulated ones. As noted in the previous chapter, the cell phone industry serves as a model of how the collective interests of individuals benefit everyone by providing more options and services. In this chapter, we are going to examine how government's interference in the free market system can hinder the best results from being attained.

For the most part, the cell phone industry has been allowed to grow and evolve without the interference of overriding governmental regulations. This simply means that the market (which consists of consumers such as you, me, and all our neighbors) has been free to decide the price, the size, the features, the plans, and all the other factors that work together to best meet the needs and desires of consumers.

A Congressional committee was never formed to make those decisions, nor did any group ever meet in an ivory tower at the Commerce Department to work out those details. We the people have evaluated our own needs. We weighed all the options available to us and made our decisions. We as consumers have, so to speak, cast our votes with the purchases we have made; while other citizens, through their businesses, have provided the options and delivered the product. Together we have helped make this product available and affordable to all, while building an industry that is a thriving segment of our economy today.

The result has been truly astounding. In a matter of minutes, we can walk into a store, find a cell phone in virtually any color or size we desire, and subscribe to a service that provides every conceivable combination of features and options that our minds can imagine. In fact, the choices are becoming hard to keep up with and so numerous that it is doubtful we should even call them phones any longer. On our cell phones today, we can store numbers, write emails, send text messages, watch movies, take pictures, listen to music, find ourselves on a real-time GPS, and, oh yes, even make a phone call if we want to. I will not be surprised if next week cell phones will help us brush our teeth and clean our houses! Just as important as the expanding features we have come to enjoy, is the shrinking prices. Cell phones have become so affordable that even my twelve-year-old son can afford a text plan on his phone - a phone that he bought himself and pays for each month!

Why is this technology so cutting edge and affordable at the same time? The answer is simple: it is because the government, for the most part, has stayed out of the way. They have let the people decide what they wanted and how much they would pay for it. When we allow the free market to work like this, people will exercise their entrepreneurial ingenuity and take risks to try new things. Some will succeed, some will fail, but that is exactly how the system works.

Can you imagine if wireless phones had been regulated in the same way that we regulated landlines? Congress would have prevented competition and choice, subsidized bad ideas while taxing good ones, broken up successful companies, and in essence chosen who would succeed and who would fail.

When comparing the advances made in the unregulated wireless phone market with that of the regulated landline market, consider how just one area of innovation would have been wiped out, had it been subjected to governmental oversight. Most of us now enjoy the convenience of some sort of wireless hands-free earpiece to use with our phones. Again, the choices we have are varied when it comes to selecting the type of device we want and the amount we are willing to pay. However, we can be sure that if bureaucrats had been involved we would all have the same, overpriced, five-pound earpiece strapped to our heads with a wrap-around headband made of Velcro. Whenever the government gets involved, the results are less than beneficial.

## Subsidizing Failure

The reason for this is twofold. First, one way that government intervention upsets the working of the free market is because they step in and prop up failing businesses. This sounds noble, but it really is not. Instead of allowing failures to occur (a very natural course within any industry), the government subsidizes failing companies and products by taking money out of the pockets of consumers and any successful competitors. Artificially supporting those who are no longer competitive prevents innovation and hurts the free market process.

The second way that government's involvement works against the free market is that it creates an environment where businesses are looking to the government rather than the marketplace for their motivation. Such a controlled atmosphere hinders entrepreneurship and rewards failure.

Unlike the free market, the government's hand is far from invisible. The positive results that come when individuals are free to exercise their own choices and decisions in an unregulated market *far* exceed those we have seen from markets that have been regulated virtually to death. If we want results that will benefit the entire community, the best thing to do is to allow the marketplace to work without interference.

Our Founding Fathers understood that governmental control of the marketplace would strip us of our individual rights, and leave us economically and morally bankrupt. We will have less research, risk, and motivation; fewer competitors and options; and a slower economy if we allow bureaucratic involvement to continue encroaching upon our free market system. This course is bad for every American, with the possible exception of the politician who keeps his or her powerbase and perks by repeating slogans such as, *"It isn't fair"* or *"Some people are making too much money,"*[59]in an effort to garner support for their socialist-leaning agendas. (No truer reflection of elitism can be found than an elected official who claims to know better than the market how much an individual should make for the product or service they provide.)

We should not be fooled into thinking that the impact such control will have on our economy will be any less harmful because it resides in the hands of our own Washington bureaucrats rather than a socialist dictator, like Venezuela's Hugo Chavez, or a group of "party leaders" such as those in the former Soviet Kremlin. A handful of American-born Ivy League graduates trying to save our nation, and the world, by imposing their "informed" decisions upon the rest of us will create the same negative results. A "controlled" economy, (regardless of who is in control) will produce the same ration lines in our country as those the people of Venezuela now stand in to buy their bread and milk.

Economic principles know no borders and they do not care what the product or industry is. They work the same across the board. Whether we are talking about cell phones or cars, milk or bread, or yes, even oil or insurance, when government picks the winners and losers and decides how much profit is too much, EVERYONE loses.

If a socialist leaning politician gets his or her way and is given the power to determine the definition of a "fair" profit level, what exactly will be the mechanism by which they will limit that profit and take away the excess? And once they have such authority, what is to keep them from deciding that YOUR salary is too high?

One of the presidential hopefuls in the 2008 election, (indeed, the front runner in 2007) revealed their core beliefs about the role of government in the following statements:

*I certainly think the free-market has failed.*[60]

*The unfettered free market has been the most radically disruptive force in American life in the last generation.*[61]

*We're going to take things away from you on behalf of the common good.*[62]

President Reagan warned us against such radical philosophy. He said:

*The Founding Fathers knew a government can't control the economy without controlling people. And they knew when a government sets out to do that, it must use force and coercion to achieve its purpose.*[63]

Thomas Jefferson also believed that such action on the part of government was inherently against the principles of freedom, saying:

*To take from one because, it is thought that his own industry and that of his father's has acquired too much, in order to spare to others who, or whose fathers have not exercised equal industry and skill, is to violate arbitrarily the first principle of association, "the guarantee to everyone of a free exercise of his industry, and the fruits acquired by it."*[64]

In other words, if people choose to associate, interact, or join forces as a community, state, or nation, the first principle they must respect is not to take away each other's profit or tell each other how to use the proceeds of their hard work. Every time a government agency tells you how to spend your money, take care of your property, raise your children, and run your business, they are violating this basic principle of association.

The problem is that you will always have certain members of a society who think they are smarter than the rest of us. They believe it is their calling in life to save us from ourselves and our own decisions. They eventually give up trying to tell us what to do through advice and start using the power of government to force us to act the way they think is best. They remove the decision making power from the individual and place it in the hands of the government, and they always profess to do it in the name of our "best interests" or "common good." They try to fool us with their cleverly crafted rhetoric, claiming that they are doing this for us, but in reality. President Reagan could see these folks coming from a mile away. He warned,

> *Public servants say, always with the best of intentions, 'What greater service we could render if only we had a little more money and a little more power.' But the truth is that outside of its legitimate function, government does nothing as well or as economically as the private sector.*[65]

The bottom line is this: one must either believe the private sector (the free market) is the best determinant of winners and losers, or that government bureaucrats can do a better job of that than we, the people. Those are the only two choices. Or, as President Reagan would say,

> *This is the issue of this election: Whether we believe in our capacity for self-government or whether we abandon the American Revolution and confess that a little intellectual elite in a far-distant capital can plan our lives for us better than we can plan them ourselves.*[66]

# 12
# THE GUARDIAN OF LIBERTY

On *WallBuilders Live!* we approach every cultural issue from two perspectives: 1) What does the Bible teach about it, and 2) What can we learn from the pages of history? On the issue of "the pursuit of happiness," the Bible is clear, and we learn from history that our Founders understood and agreed with those same biblical principles.

From a Scriptural perspective, profit is a desirable thing. It is the love of money (not money itself) that we are warned to guard against. In the parable of the talents in Matthew 25:14-30, one servant was called wicked because he was slothful and unprofitable. His talent was taken away and given to the servant who had been the most profitable. At first glance, it looks as though God is taking from the poor and giving to the rich - a Robin Hood reversal. But that is not the case.

Some people have a problem with the master giving the talent to the one who had already turned his five talents into ten. But, who better to manage the extra talent than the servant who was most prosperous? It is considered fair, in God's kingdom, to reward the most profitable servants with more. Incentive is a noble motivation to work harder. An industrious worker enjoys a just reward for their labors: it is instilled in our nature - a God-given trait.

This is why government programs that seek to do the opposite, by redistributing money from the wealthy into the government's control and then out to the poor, actually work against those it is trying to help and ruins economic vitality. The poor would be far better off if the wealthy were allowed to keep and manage their own money. History bears that fact out. When those who have the resources, are free to use that money to take care of the poor directly, through their preferred church or charity, they do a much better job than any government program has ever done.

The profit motive literally lays the foundation for a successful society. Sound crazy? Benjamin Franklin tells us, *"Industry and constant employment are great preservatives of the morals and virtue of a nation."*[67]

Can that be right? Is Franklin actually saying free market economic principles have something to do with even the *"morals and virtues"* of our nation? Yes, that is exactly what he is saying. He also said, *"There cannot be a stronger natural right than that of a man's making the best profit he can of the natural produce of his lands, provided he does not thereby hurt the state in general."*[68]

Free competitive enterprise is literally the guardian of our liberty. A free market is necessary for us to establish and maintain our freedom entire, and it is essential to passing that freedom on to the next generation.

Notice also that he says morality is tied to the free market. Recall in Chapter 10 the quote from Franklin, who said the free market is *"...the means, under God, of recovering and establishing the freedom of our country entire, and of handing it down complete to posterity."*[69] He recognized where the gift came from - it came from God. This is essential. Freedom can only be lived out when we have a respect for its Source. When we take God out of the equation, we end up with corporate corruption, greed, and Enron scandals. When moral absolutes and standards for right and wrong do not govern commerce, and instead each person is doing what seems right in his own eyes, then our market is no longer operating "under God" and corruption ensues.

## The Sum of Good Government

Thomas Jefferson said,

*A wise and frugal government, which shall restrain men from injuring one another, shall leave them otherwise free to regulate their own pursuits of industry and improvement, and shall not take from the mouth of labor the bread it has earned. This is the sum of good government.*[70]

He believed that the sum of good government came down to two basic things: deregulation and low taxes! If a company sells an inferior product, the market will take care of it by putting them out of business. If they sell a good product and make a tremendous amount of money, it is wrong for the government to take that bread away from the one who earned it in order to give it to someone else.

This is why the freedom to fail is essential for us to have the freedom to succeed. You cannot have one without the other. If you remove the freedom to fail, then you must take bread from the mouth of those who are prosperous and industrious in order to prop up those who are not. Such a socialistic state only serves to spread the misery and prevent those under its rule from enjoying the freedom to succeed.

# 13

# BUT I HATED ECONOMICS 101!

Some might say, *"I am no economist. I hated that stuff in high school and college, why should I care about it now?"* Let me give just three basic reasons why every American should care about the economy and preserving this piece of freedom's framework.

First, because our free market in America - the competitive enterprise system known as capitalism - is a fundamental pillar of our success both nationally and personally.

Without it, freedom's frame will crumble.

We have the greatest military power in the history of the world because our free market finances that military. We have achieved amazing scientific advancements and breakthrough medical technologies, things unimaginable even fifty years ago because our free market called for and financed those pursuits.

Second, (simply and selfishly) because our personal choices and the quality of our lives depend upon the continuation of our free market system. This is something many Americans rarely connect. We take for granted and choose to ignore the fact that the free market is what affords us the freedom and opportunity to make all kinds of choices about how we live our lives. Such as: the kind of automobile we drive, the electronics we buy, the food we eat, the neighborhood we live in, the music we listen to, the entertainment we enjoy, the schooling we are able to give our children (oh wait, the freedom of choice in education is not enjoyed by most Americans, though it should be), and the list goes on.

Third, because our own personal economic success depends upon the continuation of our country's free market system. Without it, we will no longer be able to exercise our God-given right to live a life in pursuit of happiness.

Sure, philosophically you may agree that it makes perfect sense, but practically speaking some may be thinking, "Hey, why all the alarm? I am doing just fine and the market is working, so why do I need to do anything differently?" My friend, never before in our nation's history have we seen such blatant efforts by certain politicians to shift us from being a country who operates under strong free market principles, to one that is more "controlled" or "managed" by government regulatory guidelines. (These are just code words for the socialist agendas that are creeping into the halls of Congress and our state legislatures.)

The unalienable right of every human being to "the pursuit of happiness" can only be experienced when there is a market that is free from government control. When government infringes upon the free competitive enterprise of its people, their rights are taken away. Yet, too often in America today, power-seeking politicians desire to implement changes that will destroy the guardian of liberty—our free market—that has fueled the engine of America's unprecedented success.

This part of the frame has been seriously undermined by a domino effect that is directly tied to the failure of our educational system by not teaching our children the basic principles of American freedom. As a result, far too many Americans today lack understanding of the importance of maintaining a truly free market. This in turn has resulted in leaders being elected who believe in draconian government controls and interference in the free marketplace.

If you think I'm exaggerating, here are just a few more quotes from a U.S. Senator, who came extremely close to winning the nomination for president in 2008. Unfortunately, these remarks represent the ideology of many of our current elected officials, in both parties:

*It's time for a new beginning, for an end to government of the few, by the few, and for the few ... And to replace it with shared responsibility for shared prosperity.*[71]

*I think it's time to send a clear message to what has become the most profitable sector in (the) entire economy that they are being watched.*[72]

The arrogance of elitism comes through in these statements. Nothing I write could better express what needs to happen in our country than the words Dr. Kenneth McFarland shared during a speech he gave at the Fairmont Hotel in San Francisco thirty years ago.

*Those in government must assume their correct role as the servants of the people and not the master. It's no secret that the government in Washington has gone literally berserk with power. Somebody said to me yesterday, they just spend money like drunken sailors and I said no, they don't. Drunken sailors spend their own money. I not long ago read a facsimile copy of the original Declaration of Independence, it was in Jefferson's handwriting. And in the very first sentence, he speaks of a "decent respect for the opinions of mankind." I wish I could address both Houses of Congress just on that text. What is meant by a "decent respect for the opinions of mankind." But Jefferson states that a "decent respect for the opinions of mankind" requires that the colonists state the reasons which compel them to separate from the Mother Country. Then he states a long list of grievances against King George, III. And will you listen carefully to this one:*

*He has erected a multitude of new offices and sent hither swarms of officers to harass our people and eat out their substance.*[73]

*Now, our forefathers revolted because they wouldn't tolerate that. And what we're tolerating today from our own government makes King George the Third look like a piker. The slogan of the Revolutionary War, you remember, taxation without representation is tyranny. Well, in the name of heaven, look what we have now with representation. I mean we're going to have to have another revolution, but this time we don't do it with bullets, we can do it with ballots - if we start now.*[74]

Will we start? Will you? Will we together answer the call to do our duty in preserving and implementing the revolutionary strategies which forged the framework of freedom we now enjoy? Will we preserve them for our children? Free competitive enterprise is the guardian of our liberty, and today the guardian needs protecting.

*If we wish to be free, if we mean to preserve inviolate those inestimable privileges for which we have been so long contending, if we mean not basely to abandon the noble struggle in which we have been so long engaged, and which we have pledged ourselves never to abandon until the glorious object of our contest shall be obtained—we must fight!*

—**Patrick Henry**

# 14

# PROTECTING THE GUARDIAN FROM THE WOLVES AT THE DOOR

What we must do is choose leaders who have faith in the framework that has made us successful as a nation. When a candidate is doubtful of the market and leans towards government controls, even when they do so in the name of preventing something "unfair" from happening, we should run as fast as we can to support someone else who would not, as a solution, seek to impose regulatory controls on our economic independence.

How do we know whether a candidate truly believes in the free market? Normally I say ignore the rhetoric and look at how they actually vote. Just like our mothers told us, it is not what you *say*...it is what you *do* that counts! The sure fire test is to watch how they vote.

Another way to tell what a candidate's core convictions are is by watching their knee jerk reaction to the issues. Study their instincts and you will see whether they believe in freedom or control? For instance, if gas prices go up, and they immediately start calling for investigations into private businesses or demanding a "windfall profits tax" to take money away from private businesses, you have a pretty good indication that they have no faith in the free market, and therefore no faith in freedom. Milton Friedman said:

*What most people really object to when they object to a free market is that it is so hard for them to shape it to their own will. The market gives people what the people want instead of what other people think they ought to want. At the bottom of many criticisms of the market economy is really lack of belief in freedom itself.*[75]

## Educational Choice

This maxim is even more obvious in the area of educational choice. Those opposed to freedom of choice in education either have zero faith in the free market to improve the product (education), or they have zero faith in their own version of the product and are afraid of competition.

If the first is true, they should take their socialistic tendencies and move elsewhere. If the second is true, well, they should still move elsewhere because their inferior product is handicapping generations of American students.

Before addressing the specifics of this issue, it should be noted that teachers are not the main problem. Most of these men and women are professionals who have dedicated their lives to the betterment of our children. They work long hours, are challenged with incredible odds and impossible situations, often without receiving the support they need and deserve from parents and/or administrators. Because of this, many of our nation's best educators are leaving the profession out of frustration.

Most objections to school choice do not come from the teachers who are in the classroom each day and who know and care about the level of education our children are receiving. Such teachers want every child to have an opportunity to get the best education possible, regardless of whether the family chooses a public, private, or charter school. The objections to school choice are most loudly voiced by misleading politicians propagating a fraud on their constituents and by entrenched bureaucratic educationalists "educrats" who simply care more about the money than they do the child.

Consider some of the objections to school choice. The number one statement is "It will hurt the public schools." To which my reply is always, "How?"

The answer that inevitably comes back is, "It will take money away from public schools."

It then becomes necessary to share with them a little bit of basic economics, and how a free market works. If consumers have a choice and the market starts "taking money away" from one provider of a product, by purchasing it from another, a reason for that shift must exist. However, preventing people from being able to make the change, neither addresses the problem nor provides a solution that is in the best interests of all concerned. In fact, it protects an inferior product, which only continues to get more inferior because there is no competition forcing it to improve.

## Competition Works

While consumers may have differing reasons for wanting change, it is ultimately because they believe that a new provider will deliver a better product. If that turns out to be untrue, the consumer can always go back to the original provider or find another.

Best of all, if many consumers leave, the public school provider will be forced to look at what they are doing wrong and how they can improve their product. Everywhere school choice has been implemented, ALL the children benefited because those who chose non-public schools received an education fitting their needs, and those who stayed in the public school experienced a better education as the public school improved in response to the competition.

The challenge to applying these basic economic principles of free enterprise in the area of education is threefold.

First, too many politicians and "educrats" do not see parents and students as the customers and the education as the product. Education elites tend to see the student as the product. From their lofty position, these social planners often believe they know what is best and are entitled to mold and shape the student to their liking, or according to what they believe the student should become, almost as if the student was a ward of the state.

In a free market, the correct view is exactly the opposite. The educational system, as the product, would be modified, molded, and shaped to meet the needs and desires of the customers, just as any other product.

Second, too many people have lost faith that the market will produce a better product. Once again, they believe in draconian control rather than choice and freedom. They just cannot let go of their tidy, top down control and allow the sometimes messy competitive process, which is fostered by a free market atmosphere, work. If they did, we would see all kinds of wonderful options and innovations in education. The different needs of children would be met, rather than the cookie cutter approach we currently have towards education, expecting each child to learn in the exact same way.

Third, a monopoly is always going to try and protect itself. Currently, our nation's public education system is a monopoly that has a powerful grip, and no intention of letting go without a fight. We, the people, must force them to release their death hold on the training of our children's minds and allow parents the freedom to choose the educational institution that they feel is best for their own children.

This is no easy task. The education monopoly is huge. And it has access to our own tax dollars, which it uses against us. Teacher salaries paid by taxpayers help fund teacher unions, and hundreds of millions of dollars are spent by them to lobby against school choice. Even those teachers who support the idea of school choice (because they understand the end-result will mean better educational choices for students and increased salaries for good teachers) are forced to fund the campaign against it because they cannot direct how their union dues are being spent.

The schools use our tax dollars to advertise for bond issues and send school officials to the legislature to lobby for more money, even while they are on the clock—being paid by taxpayer dollars. Last time I checked, they were hired to educate children, not serve as lobbyists.

But despite the odds being stacked against us, it still can be done. We can require that our candidates support freedom of choice in education before we support them in the election. Then afterwards, we can hold their feet to the fire until we see the promised changes begin to happen.

When we finally allow American ingenuity and competitive spirit into the classroom, we will have the best education system in the world in a very short time.

And, by fully implementing the revolutionary strategy of free competitive enterprise within our educational system, we will protect the guardian of our liberty by instilling these principles through our education system not only by what is taught, but also by the living example of the system itself, thriving in a competitive atmosphere

Whether in education or any other arena, free enterprise will always be the best choice. When we choose patriots, instead of politicians, as our elected officials, we will begin to see those changes take place, and our schools will begin to thrive.

## Is Freedom Fair?

Our capitols are full of politicians who promise everything and do nothing except give away what is not theirs to give. Those who do so usually do it while sounding noble. They tell us about the wrongs they want to right, and how their action is vital in making sure that something unfair will not be allowed to occur. This is usually the same argument they use against freedom and choice in education, that somehow the principles that solidified our independence, will be unfair if introduced into the training of our children. This brings me to my favorite quote of all:

*'Fair' is in the eye of the beholder; free is the verdict of the market. The word 'free' is used three times in*

*the Declaration of Independence and once in the First Amendment to the Constitution, along with 'freedom.' The word 'fair' is not used in either of our founding documents.[76]*

—**Milton Friedman**

The actions of a free market may not seem fair to some, but the solution of introducing more government control to somehow level the playing field will never produce better results. Government becoming the single determinant can only result in more who say the game is not being played fair. The beauty of the free market is that the outcome, or "verdict" as Friedman calls it above, is reached by the fairest means of all because it is a collective answer, every interested party has the opportunity to voice their opinions through their own choices and purchases. Even if they do not agree with the outcome, they have had a say in its determination.

Today, allowing government to encroach upon our free market system is the unfortunate solution that is being touted by both republicans and democrats alike, who are claiming to be able to "fix" the market. However, temporary bailouts are not lasting solutions, in fact, they only hinder the process. Only by allowing the natural process of market corrections to occur will permanent results be produced.

Take for instance, the mortgage crisis. What happened to get us in this mess is that too many borrowers wanted more of a house than their budget would allow, and too many lenders were willing to make the risky loans. Now, who is to blame for that? And what is the right solution to the problem?

The wrong solution is that we would be asked to pay for the bad decisions that were made by others. Yet, that is exactly what we are being asked to do. Congress is bailing out the lenders and borrowers who made those bad decisions, and they are going to take the money right out of your bank account and mine in order to do it.

I do not recall making a trip to the bank to co-sign for all those high-risk loans. Did you make that trip? I think not. Yet, instead of placing the blame with the two parties making the bad decision, we are left holding the bag.

Our government has decided that rather than allowing people and companies to suffer the consequences of their actions; i.e., scaling down their home choices or writing off bad debts, the government is riding in to the rescue. Members of Congress go on television and sound compassionate, but in reality, they are slowly taking away our freedom and bankrupting us all.

Think of the long-term implications of these responses. If we bail people and companies out for their bad decisions, will they be more or less likely to make the same bad decisions in the future? Any parent who has raised a child knows the answer!

If the negative consequences for a bad decision are removed, then it is no longer perceived by the person to be a bad decision. Why not do it again? The government will bail me out! So, the long-term result is a distortion in the marketplace. Rather than people learning from their bad decisions and going on to make good decisions, and allowing the "invisible hand" to have a positive impact, the opposite occurs. When you replace the "pursuit" of happiness with a guarantee of happiness, you destroy the very principles that make the system work.

*We who live in free market societies believe that growth, prosperity and ultimately human fulfillment, are created from the bottom up, not the government down. Only when the human spirit is allowed to invent and create, only when individuals are given a personal stake in deciding economic policies and benefiting from their success—only then can societies remain economically alive, dynamic, progressive, and free. Trust the people.*

**—Ronald Reagan**
*September 29, 1981*

President Reagan said it best: either we trust that the free market (i.e. you and me) is capable of making choices that serve the best interests of the whole nation, or we must put our trust in government bureaucrats to make those decisions for us. Who is better qualified?

## FRAMEWORK #4
### Consent of the Governed

*The American war is over; but this is far from being the case with the American revolution. On the contrary, nothing but the first act of the drama is closed. It remains yet to establish and perfect our new forms of government, and to prepare the principles, morals, and manners of our citizens for these forms of government after they are established and brought to perfection.*

—**Benjamin Rush**
*Letter to Price*
*May 25, 1786*

# 15

# LIVES, FORTUNES, AND SACRED HONOR

We each have a duty and responsibility to preserve freedom by participating in the process, even though sometimes that requires sacrifice. Before we discuss the very small sacrifices required of us today, we can gain perspective by considering the sacrifice of those who came before us.

It is hard to imagine what was going through the minds of those 56 men as they gathered over 230 years ago to sign the Declaration of Independence. John Hancock, who served as President of Congress, and Charles Thomson, who was the Secretary, are the only two who actually signed the Declaration on July 4th, 1776, the date we commemorate our nation's independence. Most of the rest of the delegates placed their signatures on the document almost a month later, August 2nd.[i]

---

[i] To be completely accurate, only 53 more would sign on this particular day as Matthew Thornton and Thomas McKean would not sign until October and November, respectively. Charles Thomson, though an important patriot leader and Secretary of Congress, is not counted as one of the 56 delegates who signed.

Each of the Signers who gathered that day must have been felt mixed emotions. On one hand, the Declaration of Independence validated all their hopes and dreams for a new and independent nation - the likes of which the world had never seen before. On the other, they understood that a defeat to the British army (which was very likely) would mean that they were essentially signing their own death certificates on that momentous day.

A silence filled the room as Secretary Thomson began the session. He read the names of each of the signers who were present that day, and one-by-one they came forward. He started with the delegation seated to his right, New Hampshire. The first man called was Josiah Bartlett, who rose in what Benjamin Rush would later describe as a "pensive silence,"[77] and made his way to the front of the room. He picked up the quill, dipped it in the silver inkwell (still in Independence Hall today), and signed his name.

In the same manner, each man came forward. The scratching of the quill upon the surface of the parchment was the only sound heard as each man affixed his name to the bottom of the Declaration of Independence.

Only when Elbridge Gerry of Massachusetts came forward was the silence finally broken. Mr. Gerry, who would later become Vice President during the presidency of James Madison, was a small man in stature. As he was signing the Declaration of Independence, Benjamin Harrison, (one of the largest of the Founding Fathers) could not resist the opportunity to break the tension.

To fully appreciate the levity, picture the scene. The smallest man in the room is in front signing what amounts to a warrant for the arrest and execution of everyone present, when from the rear of the room, the guy who could play middle linebacker for the Cowboys, blurts out:

> *I shall have a great advantage over you, Mr. Gerry, when we are all hung for what we are now doing. From the size and great weight of my body, I shall die in a few minutes, but from the lightness of yours, you will dance in the air for an hour or two before you are dead.*[78]

Every man in the room appreciated the humor. They all knew what was at stake. Yet without hesitation, they picked up the pen, dipped it in the ink, and scratched their names directly below the amazing final sentence, which reads:

> *For the support of this Declaration, with a firm reliance on the protection of Divine Providence, we mutually pledge to each other our Lives, our Fortunes and our Sacred Honor.* [79]

These men were true American patriots; they all kept their word. Each of them made personal sacrifices for the freedom we enjoy. Many literally gave their lives, fortunes, and sacred honor to the cause of American independence.

As we embark upon our duty to live out this principle, "consent of the governed," let us learn how, from the examples of these men. I want to recommend two great resource if you want to delve deeper into each of their stories. WallBuilders produces a reprint of an 1848 textbook entitled, *Lives of the Signers*. It can be purchased on our website at www.wallbuilders.com.

My friend, Mark Cole, has written another great resource, *Lives, Fortunes, and Sacred Honor*, which details each of the signer's lives, the sacrifices they made, and most importantly, the lessons we can learn and emulate from each of them. I highly recommend it. You can find his book online at www.amazon.com.

# 16

# RENDER HONOR UNTO WHOM HONOR IS DUE

Our Founding Fathers were not super heroes. They were ordinary men, sinners, like you and me, who rose to infamy during extraordinary times. They were true patriots and heroes, not because they signed a document, but because they backed up their word with their lives.

Not one of them turned back, despite the hard battles they all faced. Some watched their homes go up in smoke; others lost fortunes overnight; their sons went off to war never to return home again; a few even laid down their own lives on the frontlines. Together, they lit the torch of freedom and passed it on intact to their children.

Since then, each generation of Americans has done the same. They have been willing to pay the ultimate price to ensure and defend American freedom. All of them, from 1776 to today, are worthy of honor. In John 15:13, Jesus said, *"Greater love has no one than this, than to lay down one's life for his friends."*[80]

Each generation of Americans has had a remnant of bold citizens who willingly made that ultimate sacrifice of love to preserve our nation's freedom. These men and women deserve our utmost respect and honor. Abraham Lincoln said it best,

*It is from these honored dead that we take increased devotion to the cause for which they gave the last full measure of devotion; that we highly resolve that these dead shall not have died in vain, that this nation under God shall have a new birth of freedom, and that government of the people, by the people, for the people shall not perish from the earth.*[81]

In Romans 13:7, we are instructed to render honor to whom honor is due. Unfortunately, sacrifice and civic duty is not something held in high esteem these days. But, I can think of no group of Americans more worthy of our honor than those who serve our country, whether in the military or even at home in civil service roles, such as that of our police and fire fighters. They all deserve our honor.

## Welcome Home

I recently learned that at airports across America, wherever thousands of troops are returning home to American soil, a group called *Operation Welcome Home a Hero*, are doing just that. They are honoring those who deserve our honor by giving these returning soldiers a hero's welcome. What began at Dallas Fort Worth airport in Texas has also spread to Atlanta, Georgia, and Bangor, Maine. As troops return, they are greeted by the cheers of hundreds of Americans gathered in their honor. A victory line is formed that the troops walk through and rarely a dry eye can be found. This happens almost every single day of the year.

You may not be able to come out and join them, but the next time you see an American soldier, walk over and shake their hand. Let them know how much their personal sacrifice is appreciated, and that many in America are praying for their safety. They will be honored, and it will bless your day as well!

# 17

# LIVING LIVES WORTHY OF THE SACRIFICE MADE FOR US

If you saw the movie, *Saving Private Ryan*, you will recall the ending scene where Captain Miller gives his own life to save the life of this young man. All of Private Ryan's brothers had been killed in action, and Captain Miller was assigned the task of bringing this family's only remaining son off the front lines and safely home. He gave his life in the process, but with his final breath, Captain Miller pulled Private Ryan close and whispered two powerful words: "Earn this." He then died in Private Ryan's arms. The very next scene shows Private Ryan, roughly sixty years later, kneeling at the grave of Captain Miller. In a quiet voice, he expresses the hope that the life he lived had somehow been worthy of the sacrifice made.

That closing scene had a powerful impact on me - it made the cost of freedom personal. I sobbed, as I sat in the theater and wondered if the life I was living was worthy of the price that has been paid.

Whenever I am tempted to take for granted the privileges given to me as a citizen of this amazing nation, that scene comes back to mind. If I am feeling too tired or disinterested to get out and vote or take on a worthy cause, I think of all those who have paid the ultimate price, and I ask myself, "Am I really living a life worthy of their sacrifice? Do I deserve the freedom that I've been given?"

A true American patriot lives their life today in a way that honors the past sacrifice that others have made. Those who have gone before have given much so we could have the freedom to vote for our leaders and pray for our nation. Are we willing to give the fifteen minutes daily it takes to exercise those privileges?

Remember, our Founding Fathers pledged their *Lives, Fortunes, and Sacred Honor* to each other and to the cause of freedom. What is being asked of us today is that we would honor their sacrifice by exercising our freedoms and ensuring they are not lost to future generations of Americans.

Today, giving of our lives, fortunes, and sacred honor is more of a privilege than a sacrifice.

*Lives:* Are we willing to give the little time needed to vote, pray, and carry out our civic responsibilities?

*Fortunes:* Are we willing to give a small portion of our finances to causes and candidates that will defend the principles and strategies of freedom that have made our nation great?

***Sacred Honor:*** Are we willing to stand against the opposition by writing a letter to the editor, running for office, or showing up to speak out at the next School Board meeting? The insults hurled at us are nothing compared to the bullets taken by those who came before us.

The torch of freedom is not a self-sustaining flame; it must be guarded, and it must be instilled in each generation. We honor those who protected our freedom in the past by doing our part today. The question is: have we earned it?

# 18

# *CLEAN* THE HOUSE,
# DON'T ABANDON IT

It took approximately one hundred years for the principles of freedom embodied in the heart of the Declaration of Independence to be granted to all Americans regardless of race, creed, or gender. The expansion of freedom in our nation's history resulted from men and women who understood the idea of self-government established by the founders and got involved in the process of making that a reality for every American. The Declaration of Independence would be nothing more than an archaic document today, if not for the men and women who dared to live by what it says.

*We hold these truths to be self-evident, that all men are created equal, that they are endowed by their Creator with certain unalienable Rights, that among these are Life, Liberty and the pursuit of Happiness. That to secure these rights, Governments are instituted among Men, deriving their just powers from the consent of the governed.*[82]

From the start, the frame found in those precious fifty-six words in the heart of the Declaration of Independence would have amounted to nothing more than a hoped for ideology. It was the actions of the fifty-six Signers who embraced those ideals that turned them into a living reality. Our Founding Fathers had the faith to back up what they believed with action. We must do the same today.

We know the importance of faith in action. The Bible reminds in James 2:26 that *"As the body without the spirit is dead, so faith without works is dead also."*[83] What good is freedom of religion if we are not exercising our faith in *every* arena?

One action that should be taken within the Christian community is a reversal of the mindset that encourages a divide between the secular and spiritual aspects of our lives. This split mentality has only served one purpose - to neuter the voice of people of faith and remove us from having a positive influence on our culture.

I am always hearing from good, godly people who tell me that they do not want to get involved in politics because of all the unethical, evil, and corrupt people in that arena. Believe me, I know the truth of that from personal experience, but that fact only reinforces the reason why Christians ought to be taking more of a role in the process of governing our nation.

## It is a Blood Sport

When I first decided to run for the legislature, I was warned about the lies that would inevitably be written in the newspapers about me since I had thrown my hat into this political arena. However, even with the benefit of foreknowledge and warnings, I was not fully prepared for the deliberate malicious attacks that were later unleashed by my opponent during my 2002 re-election campaign for Texas State Representative.

As a conservative republican in a 50/50 district, in a year when control of the legislature was up for grabs, I became the number one target of the Texas Democratic Party. Before it was all over, they had spent $1.2 million dollars to defeat me. When you compare this to my $300,000 campaign budget, you get an idea of the all out war that was being waged.

None of this surprised me; I had been warned it could get nasty. However, what I did not expect was the number of corruption claims that were hurled against me. During the heat of the final ten days of the campaign, a liberal Austin newspaper ran headline stories almost daily reporting a number of alleged criminal investigations that the local prosecutor's office was preparing against me. At the time, it all seemed a little too coordinated to me, but since I was the one under attack, I did not want to let my suspicions turn to paranoia, so I decided to try to spend what was left of the campaign focused on the issues.

However, once the election was over and my opponent was safely tucked away in the State House, all the allegations amazingly went away. No charges were ever filed and the lead prosecutor on my "case" during the campaign gave up his government job to go to work for one of my opponent's largest contributors.

Yes, the political world can be a corrupt environment at times. I have experienced the dirty side firsthand, but I look at it this way. When our sons play in mud puddles, my wife does not abandon the boys; she simply washes away the dirt. When the house gets dirty, we do not move; we get out the disinfectant and start scrubbing. The political arena is no different. Rather than walking away from it because some have muddied the waters, we need to roll up our sleeves and get to work cleaning up the mess. After all, this is our home. Our government belongs to us. It was designed to operate by the consent of the governed and the reason we do not see more of God's principles at work in the political arena is simply because not enough Christians are taking part in the process. Too many have walked away and left the other kids playing in the mud!

For most of the latter part of the twentieth century, Christians have done just that. We have sat on our hands, safe in our church pews and left it up to someone else to take care of running the government. Guess what? Somebody else has. Without a strong Christian presence, our nation and even the world have been affected by a variety of postmodern, humanistic, and godless philosophies that are threatening to strip us of our freedoms.

If we are looking for someone to blame for the moral decay of America today, we need look no further. As Christians, we share in the responsibility for much of the godlessness that exists in our world today. We have the same unique opportunity as every American, to have a voice in our nation's government, yet we have chosen to remain silent. We are the ones who have abdicated our civic responsibilities, en masse. John Hancock, who was one of the Founders largely responsible for the early days of the American Revolution, said:

> *I conjure you, by all that is dear, by all that is honorable, by all that is sacred; not only that ye pray, but that ye act.*[84]

In the Sermon on the Mount, Jesus asked His followers, "What good is salt that has lost its flavor?" "What good is light that is hidden away, never shining in this dark world?" We need to ask those same questions today. We, the people of God, are His ambassadors in our world and He is asking the same questions of us - where is the salt and light?

## Change is Coming

However, even after saying all that, I must tell you I am optimistic for our future. I believe change is coming. Indeed, over the last ten to fifteen years, a resounding wake-up call has been ringing in the Christian community. People of faith have begun to take notice and are realizing their responsibility for our nation's current moral state. They are beginning to sense the urgency in which we need to act in response to many of the current issues and liberal political agendas that are on the table today. Such as:

- Bold initiatives by those advocating homosexual marriage to be on equal footing with traditional marriage.

- The practice of infanticide under the name of partial-birth abortion.

- The chipping away of our liberty by the courts and an over-reaching government entanglement in our personal lives.

- The education of our children. Parents are tired of being told their only options are failing public schools where the kids are fighting off guns, drugs, and gangs.

- Taxes. Homeowners are tired of watching their property taxes become more than their mortgage as they are forced to pay rent to the government, never actually owning their own property, and many being forced to sell their homes as a result.

What will be left to our children and grandchildren, unless people of faith determine today to once again be a part of the political process? We must perform our duty as stewards of the torch of freedom which has been entrusted to us.

Proverbs makes it clear that the people rejoice when the righteous rule, but the people groan when the wicked rule.[85] It could not be more plainly stated than that. Neither the righteous nor the wicked can rule in America unless "we the people" elect them. It is vitally important to have godly men and women in office who understand the foundations of freedom. And, that will not happen unless godly men and women elect them. Now is the time for all of us to get involved in the process and uphold our responsibilities.

Charles Finney, a preacher in the Second Great Awakening, said:

*Politics are part of a religion in a country such as this, and Christians must do their duty to their country as a part of their duty to God... God will bless or curse this nation, according to the course Christians take in politics.*[86]

President James Garfield, who was also a revival preacher in the Second Great Awakening, said:

*Now more than ever before, the people are responsible for the character of their Congress. If that body be ignorant, reckless, and corrupt, it is because the people tolerate ignorance, recklessness, and corruption. If it be intelligent, brave, and pure, it is because the people demand these high qualities to represent them in the national legislature.*

*If the next centennial does not find us a great nation…it will be because those who represent the enterprise, the culture, and the morality of the nation do not aid in controlling the political forces.*[87]

Who represents the enterprise, the culture, and the morality of the nation?

We do.

This is what "consent of the governed" is all about. In the next section, we will briefly explore four very basic activities through which each of us can actively give or refuse our consent.

## ACTIONS WE CAN ALL TAKE

*There is a time for all things, a time to preach and a time to pray, but those times have passed away. There is a time to fight, and that time has now come.*

**—Peter Muhlenberg**
*Excerpt from a Lutheran sermon*
*Woodstock, Virginia*
*January, 1776*

# 19

# EVERY VOTE REALLY DOES COUNT!

## Hanging Chads before They Were Cool

It was around midnight on election night in 1998, when my campaign manager brought me the news that we had been waiting for since the polls closed. The final numbers were in from the election clerks of the three counties in the Texas district where I was running for a seat in the State House of Representatives. They showed that thirty thousand people had voted in that race and I had lost by twenty votes. Twenty votes!

The guy standing next to me said, *"Twenty votes? I could have gotten you twenty more votes Rick!"* That was probably not the best timing or the wisest thing for him to say to me, but I restrained myself from laying hands on him that night (and not for prayer). But he was right. After all, twenty votes is just one *decent* size Texas home school family! Kara and I home school our four children (or I should say Kara home schools our four children) and friends who have many more children than us, like to encourage us by saying, *"Nice start you got going there!"*

As the news spread of the extremely narrow margin of votes by which I had lost the election, I began to receive hundreds of phone calls from supporters who were all asking me to request a recount. In Texas, we have a statute that authorizes a recount when a race is this close. So, at their prompting I decided to ask that the votes would be counted again.

The recount was to be done one county at a time, and we started with the most democrat county in the district. My team knew nothing about the recount process. Recall the year. This was 1998, two years before the world would learn all about recounts and hanging chads in the Florida presidential election.

I was the only attorney on the team; the rest were either family members or volunteers from my church and other churches in the district. So, you can imagine our level of intimidation when we arrived at the start of the recount and faced the incumbent's team of high-powered attorneys. But what we lacked in one area we made up for in another—we had a team who was praying around the clock, and a group of dedicated volunteers who were ready to stay as long as it took to make sure that every ballot was counted correctly.

By the end of the recount of that first county, we had picked up three votes. The next morning, we counted the second county and picked up another four votes. As I was driving over to the third county where

Kara and our family team were getting ready for the last count to begin, I started doing the math in my head.

The first two counties combined were half the size of the third county. So statistically in my mind, we should pick up twice as many votes in the third county as we did in the first two. That could mean fourteen votes added to the seven we already had for a total of twenty-one new votes in all. If so, that would mean that I could win the election by a ONE vote victory!

My mind was reeling on the way to the courthouse where the final count was to take place—I must have broken every traffic law in the book that day. When I arrived, I saw the six tables that had been set up for the recount teams. Each side was allowed to have one representative per table.

For the first half hour or so, not much happened. Then Chad Hudson, Kara's cousin, whispered to me that we had just picked up four votes at his table. A friend of the family, Brian Wittmuss, came and told me we had just picked up another five votes. Now that we were down to a margin of four votes, the attorneys on the other side were starting to sweat. They had probably assured their client—the incumbent—that a recount would not change the election because it had not happened in more than twenty years!

The whirlwind continued for the next couple of hours. Kara's aunt brought news of twelve more votes, my mother-in-law announced another ten, someone else from another table said we had just lost seven, and on it went until it was finally over, and we had picked up forty-nine additional votes in that one county. Combined with the votes we picked up in the recount of the other two counties, we had a combined total of fifty-six additional votes. This meant that I went from losing the election by twenty votes, to winning it by thirty-six.

Two months later, I took the oath of office as the youngest freshman in the Texas House of Representatives. President Bush (Governor of Texas at the time) nicknamed me *"Landslide Green,"* which he thought was very funny in 1998. However, it was probably not making him smile all that much when in the 2000 election we all had to wait for the Florida returns to be recounted to know who would be the next President of the United States. That year, the presidential election was decided by a narrow margin of 537 votes.[88]

So, never buy the lie that your one vote does not count. Voting is the best way for you to have your voice heard and your values counted. Remember, our nation does not elect the leaders that a majority of its citizens prefer. It elects the leaders that a majority of the citizens *who show up to vote* choose! If you don't vote, you don't count.

# 20

# TOGETHER WE *CAN* MAKE
# A DIFFERENCE!

*If men of wisdom and knowledge, of moderation and*
*temperance, of patience, fortitude and perseverance, of*
*sobriety and true republican simplicity of manners, of*
*zeal for the honour of the Supreme Being and the*
*welfare of the commonwealth; if men possessed of*
*these other excellent qualities are chosen to fill the*
*seats of government, we may expect that our affairs*
*will rest on a solid and permanent foundation.*

—**Samuel Adams**
*Letter to Elbridge Gerry*
*November 27, 1780*

As millions of freedom-loving Americans
become more involved in the process of self-
government, gains are being made in virtually every
corner. In fact, each week David Barton and I devote
our Friday program on *"WallBuilders Live!"* to
highlighting some of the good news reports that we
receive from many who are making a difference across

the nation. Inch by inch, those who are engaged in the culture war are winning back the courts, state legislatures, agencies, elections, local school districts, and more, from liberal politicians and socialist agendas. Not that we are without the defeats and setbacks that come with the territory—we can't win them all. But when we stay engaged in the process—aggressively, strategically, offensively, and with the long-term in view—we win.

The price of freedom is vigilance, and it is time for us to be more vigilant. We start by supporting patriots who will get the job done. We need leaders who will take action. Men and women who will follow in the example of Patrick Henry, who said:

> *"The battle, sir, is not to the strong alone; it is to the vigilant, the active, the brave..."*[89]

God gives clear instruction in the Bible, for choosing leaders. He says:

> *"Moreover you shall select from all the people able men, such as fear God, men of truth, hating covetousness."*[90]

***Able men:*** this simply means those we choose need to be qualified (able) to do the job they are being elected to do and willing to take whatever action necessary to get it done. It is time to stop supporting politicians that tell us what we want to hear, and never do what they say.

***Such as fear God*:** this means that the candidates we chose should have strong convictions and a solid Biblical worldview. I have a suspicion that the "you tube" revolution is going to catch up with some of those silver-tongued, sound-bite gurus and bring them down. We need to support candidates who have more to offer than catchy slogans, we need men and women who are the real deal and who recognize the One who is the Real Deal—Jesus—and honor Him with their words and their actions.

***Men of truth*:** this means those we support must be honest even when it hurts, regardless of whether the pain is inflicted upon themselves or others.

*"In selecting men for office, let principle be your guide. Regard not the particular sect or denomination of the candidate—look to his character...."*

**—Noah Webster**
Letters to a Young Gentleman
Commencing His Education, 1789

I respect a candidate who tells me hard truth. The one who says that it is not the proper role of our government to take money from my neighbor to solve my problem, regardless of how much he sympathizes with my problem. Even if it hurts me to hear it, an honest statesman will be the one who lays the truth out plainly and does what is best, even when it is not popular. A candidate who twists the truth, misrepresents an opponent's position, or changes his position when speaking to different audiences, is clearly not a person of truth.

**Hating covetousness:** this is probably the most difficult trait to find in an elected official or a candidate running for public office these days. President Reagan once described the two kinds of people in politics: those who want to *be* somebody and those who want to *do* something. Someone who hates covetousness is in it for the cause—they want to *do* something. They are not in it for what they can get out of it personally. We desperately need patriots who are willing to put the good of the state and the nation above their own political fortunes.

God has given us the best checklist we'll ever have for deciding how to vote. So remember, as you exercise your duty to vote, choose:

- *Able men*: Those who can, and will, do the job.

- *Such as fear God*: Those who believe in moral absolutes and recognize and honor God in their words and actions.

- *Men of truth:* Those who have a record of doing what they say.

- *Hating covetousness:* Those who are not in it for what they can get personally, but for what they can do for the cause of freedom.

It amazes me to see public officials in Washington, D.C. hitch their wagon to the defeat of America. They practically cheer when things go bad in any part of the War on Terror because it allows them to gain political ground by blaming President Bush. They forget the fact that virtually everyone in Washington, D.C. supported the war in Iraq when it first started.

What we need in these difficult times are patriots willing to stand up and do what is best for the nation, rather than look for opportunities to take cheap shots at fellow Americans in order to score political points. Such self-centered action gives aid and comfort to our enemy and demoralizes our troops.

*Republics are created by the virtue, public spirit, and intelligence of the citizens. They fall, when the wise are banished from the public councils, because they dare to be honest, and the profligate are rewarded, because they flatter the people, in order to betray them."*

**—Joseph Story**
*Commentaries on the Constitution*
*1833*

Do not choose the candidate you will vote for based solely upon what they say, look at what they have done. Consider closely their public positions and voting records. What side are they fighting on? Just as Colonel William Prescott told the troops at Bunker Hill, *"Don't fire until you see the whites of their eyes,"* you and I should not pull the lever and fire our votes until we too can see what each candidate really does, not merely what they say they will do. We do that by looking at their voting record and life experience.

Check out the local voter guides in your area (visit www.wallbuilders.com for links or go directly to www.votesmart.org and review the actual voting records of the candidates) and identify the candidate that most closely resembles your beliefs.

## Vote Smart

Choose strategically. We should not waste what we have been given. To vote for third party candidates who have no chance of winning is to waste our vote and help the other side. In the rare case where the best candidate happens to be a third party candidate AND also has a real chance of winning (which the polls will reflect), then shake things up and go for it. But please do not buy into the idea of a "protest vote." That usually results in the candidate that you disagree with the most being elected.

It is better to vote for someone who can win, even though you may only agree with them fifty percent of the time, than to vote for someone who absolutely cannot win, who you agree with ninety percent of the time. If a candidate has no hope of winning the election that means they do not meet the requirement of being "able men." Such an unwise use of your vote usually helps the candidate you disagree with the most win the race. It is better to get the best you can today and work hard to support better candidates to be on the ballot tomorrow.

People often tell me, "I just do not want to have to choose the lesser of two evils." Well, my friends, that is always the option because we are all depraved and there is no perfect candidate. Jesus is not on the ballot, so you will always have to vote for a less than perfect individual.

And finally, remember that voting is not the only way we participate in the governing of this nation. Although it is vitally important that we exercise that right and duty, showing up to vote is not the only responsibility that we have as citizens. We must do more to ensure that the freedoms we have are preserved for future generations. For some that might mean:

- Putting your own name on the ballot

- Volunteering your time to help run a campaign

- Contributing funds to support the campaigns of those whose beliefs you share

- Working as political staffers to assist elected officials

- Running agencies with a conservative perspective

- Serving as judges

- Hosting radio programs, podcasts, and blogs

- Raising up the next generation of American patriots

In 1802, Reverend Matthias Burnett made this statement, which is just as applicable to us today. He said:

> *Finally ye . . . whose power it is to save or destroy your country, consider well the important trust . . . which God . . . has put into your hands. To God and posterity, you are accountable for them. . . Let not your children have reason to curse you for giving up those rights, and prostrating those institutions which your fathers delivered to you.*[91]

# 21

# PUT YOUR MONEY WHERE YOUR VALUES ARE

*For where your treasure is, there your heart will be also.*[92]

– *Matthew 6:21*

Is your heart with America? I doubt you would have picked up this book if you did not consider yourself a patriotic American. So, we probably share similar goals of preserving freedom for future generations. However, if that describes you, let me ask you...are you putting your money where your values are? Are you willing to invest in preserving freedom for our sons and daughters by supporting the causes and candidates that will fight to preserve freedom, because the other side is certainly willing to dig deep into their pockets to finance their cause.

Recently, I interviewed a conservative Christian school board member from California on our radio program, whose story shows how far those whose hearts are not with America will go to promote their agenda. Simply because he supported displaying our country's national motto, "In God We Trust" on campus, his opponents spent over $330,000 in an effort to defeat him, an amount unheard of for a school board election! Compared to his $30,000 campaign budget, they had him outspent ten to one. Yet, he won the race!

He credits his victory to God's hand working through Christians who prayed and willingly volunteered to help him to withstand the onslaught that was unleashed against him.

But why did the other side have so much more money to spend on a seemingly insignificant school board election? Certainly, the small percentage of secular humanists in America do not have ten times as much wealth as people of faith, yet they consistently have more financial influence, because they are willing to invest in the future. They understand the importance and the cost of getting their agenda passed. This is something our side often misses.

Billionaire homosexual Tim Gill is now spending millions of dollars each election cycle to defeat pro-family candidates who support traditional marriage.[93] He has already taken out dozens of pro-family champions around the nation, while conservatives sit on their wallets and say "What a shame."

It takes money to win elections, and winning elections is how we are going to win the culture war. Some of you may never run for office, but you can do a great deal to help the cause of freedom by contributing even a small portion of your resources to the process. The Founders pledged their "fortunes" to the cause - and indeed, many gave it all, some even died in debtors' prison.

By contrast, if we would be willing to just give as much to the causes and candidates that support our beliefs as we spend on Starbucks, the good guys would have all the funds necessary.

## Talk is Cheap

No nice way of saying this, so here goes...I am tired of spoiled Americans living off the sacrifices of those who came before us and being unwilling to sacrifice anything themselves in order to preserve freedom on our watch.

I once had a businessman tell me he fully supported me for State Representative and agreed with me on virtually every issue and thought our state really needed me in the legislature. But then he let me know he could not contribute to my campaign or put a sign in his yard because he was afraid the democrats in our community might not patronize his business.

I wanted to be polite and diplomatic - I really did!

I know exactly what I should have said, something like *"Well, your vote counts the most, and I appreciate your support."* But I was in the middle of a nasty campaign. I was sacrificing virtually every night away from my family to campaign across the district. I was hurting financially because campaigning was preventing me from paying attention to my business and making money (state representative in Texas pays a whopping $600 per month).

With all of that churning around in my head and this Christian man who shared my values telling me he could not publicly support me over the pro-abortion, pro-gay rights, ultra-liberal person running against me because he might lose a sale or two, I just had to speak my mind. I said,

> *My friend, should I lose this race, when your new state representative kills the property tax relief plan I've been pushing, and he votes for all the big government programs he supports, and he brings more regulations to your business and he raises your taxes...you'll be getting exactly what you deserve because you were unwilling to take a stand. Hopefully it will not come to that. I'm going to keep sacrificing my personal finances, sacrificing time with my family, and allowing my name to be dragged through the mud...all so I can fight for the things you want, but are unwilling to fight for. Enjoy your freedom while you've got it.*

Okay, so it was not a chapter out of Carnegie's *"How to Win Friends and Influence People."* If you have made it this far into the book, you now realize why Kara so often has to tell me *"Just pause and think a little more before you speak!"*

Of course, my response to her in those situations is that I am in good company. Consider here what Samuel Adams would have said to my friend:

> *If ye love wealth better than liberty, the tranquility of servitude than the animating contest of freedom, go from us in peace. We ask not your counsels or arms. Crouch down and lick the hands that feed you. May your chains sit lightly upon you, and may posterity forget that ye were our countrymen.*[94]

Or this from Benjamin Franklin:

> *Those who would give up essential liberty, to purchase a little temporary Safety, deserve neither Liberty nor safety.*[95]

As former House Majority Leader Tom Delay likes to say, Americans spend more money on potato chips than all federal, state, and local elections combined. Some say we spend too much on elections, but the fact is we should be investing *more* in our leadership and the future of our nation.

I urge you to look for ways to invest in freedom. Tax-deductible contributions can be made to non-profit organizations like WallBuilders, the Torch of Freedom Foundation, Alliance Defense Fund, and many other local organizations in your state that are dedicated to preserving our liberty.

But do not just look for tax-deductible opportunities. We conservatives are, well, conservative about finances, and that is a good thing. However, our perspective needs some adjustment when it comes to the area of political giving. We need to realize that the ROI (return on investment) of a political gift will be enjoyed by our children, our grandchildren, and us. Give to local candidates and give to political action committees you know share your values.

If you are a successful person in business, you may not have time to investigate candidates and determine which races can be won; i.e., which races are a good investment. Political Action Committees that share your values can help you make good investments and positively influence the culture. If you are not familiar with any PACs you trust to make good decisions with your dollars, feel free to contact me through www.rickgreen.com.

If you truly love freedom, if you care whether your children and grandchildren will live in freedom, put your money where your values are and make the sacrifices necessary to keep the torch burning brightly.

# 22

# SPEAK OUT: JOIN THE DISCUSSION

Everyone has a sphere of influence. It may be five people or it may be five thousand, but each of us can speak out, participate in the debate, and be an influence on those around us. Sometimes it will be at the coffee shop or the little league game, but wherever you are, look for an opportunity to politely plant seeds of the revolutionary strategies in the lives of those you meet.

I admit that I am encouraging you to get involved for a very selfish reason. It is because I know what you do will impact and affect my children. Whether or not Trey, Reagan, Kamryn, and Rhett enjoy freedom throughout their lifetimes will depend not just on what Kara and I do, but on what you do in your community as well. We are in this together.

I know I mentioned this earlier, but it bears repeating. John Hancock, who was one of the Founders largely responsible for the early days of the American Revolution, said: *"I conjure you, by all that is dear, by all that is honorable, by all that is sacred; not only that ye pray, but that ye act.'*[96]

We need to be careful that we do not get so heavenly minded that we are of no earthly good. What I mean by that is if we stay in our prayer closet twenty-four hours a day, seven days a week, and do not fulfill our responsibilities to be salt and light within the community, we have missed our opportunity to be an influence in our world.

Some of us think that because we have the Constitution we do not need to be involved—our freedoms are already protected by the document. Here's an answer to that thinking from John Francis Mercer, a Maryland delegate to the Constitution Convention. He said,

> *It is a great mistake to suppose that the paper we are to compose will govern the United States. It is the men who we will bring into the government, and the interest they have in maintaining it that is to govern them. The paper will only mark out the mode and the form, the men are the substance and must do the business.*[97]

In *Newdow v. U.S. Congress*, the Ninth Circuit quotes only one line from the Constitution; the decision ignores the men that drafted the document and focuses on the men and women who have handed down judicial decisions during the last forty years. It does not matter how well written the Constitution or the Declaration of Independence is if we do not have men and women in office and on the bench who protect the documents and preserve the freedom those documents describe.

A perfect example is Rabbi Gutterman and *Lee v. Wiesman*,[98] the case we discussed earlier regarding prayer at a graduation. Those of us who supported prayer at graduations pointed to the actions of the Founding Fathers, such as William Samuel Johnson preaching at graduations. In his opinion, Justice Souter recognized our arguments and said in effect we were right about Founding Fathers praying at public school graduations. He then went on to say it just meant the Founding Fathers did not understand the Constitution. Clearly a ridiculous notion.

But if a Supreme Court Justice, like Justice Souter does not care about the intent of the document, what good is it? In order to defend and protect the Constitution, we need men and women in office who care about its true intent. It is our job as citizens to remove the ones who ignore original intent and replace them with those who understand and respect it.

To do that job well, we must become educated and equipped. At WallBuilders, we have a massive amount of free material on our website to help you get started. And you can listen to the program *WallBuilders Live!* every day either on your radio, or via the website. Learning about the issues of the day, and being encouraged with stories of people who are making a difference will equip you to be an influence in your community.

Encourage your church to start a "salt and light ministry." Use WallBuilders materials in your Sunday School class or start The Truth Project at your church (www.thetruthproject.org).

There is so much you can do to add to the discussion and influence the people around you. You just have to get started…today!

# 23

# DUTY IS OURS; RESULTS ARE GOD'S

Occasionally, I hear frustrated comments from conservatives who have gotten involved in the political realm over the last few years. They say things such as, "Rick, I hear what you're talking about, but I worked hard to get candidates elected and they did not do the things they promised to do."

The main reason Republicans lost majority control of the Congress in 2006 was that Christian conservatives got fed up with what they perceived as broken promises by those they elected to office. So, in droves those voters decided to sit out the election. They felt that since the Republicans they elected to Congress were acting just like the Democrats, they would show them their disapproval by staying away from the polls in protest.

The problem with that logic is that the perception they had that the leaders they worked hard to elect were no longer working on the conservative agendas they had promised to implement, was incorrect.

The reality is this. Conservatives in Congress were fighting the good fight, but they did not have the numbers they needed yet to get everything done. The Republican majority at the time only had a razor thin margin and moderate Republicans still had all the power because they could swing the vote either way. So, by sitting out the election, all the conservative Christian voters succeeded in doing was to hand the reins of Congress over to the pro-abortion, pro-gay marriage, anti-free market liberals.

Sadly, since they did not see one hundred percent of what they had wanted accomplished, as fast as they had hoped, those voters essentially took their bat and ball and got out of the game. Now, the rest of the team must fight harder to accomplish even less. The whole momentum was lost due to their ill-timed temper tantrum.

Our government does not work apart from the virtues of patience and perseverance. The better move would have been for those voters to continue to exercise their duty as citizens by voting. They also should have stayed connected with their elected officials and have taken more of a role in helping them to win those issues that were important.

Sitting out elections is never the right course of action. It is not the way our government was designed to work. We should do what we can to get the best candidates on the ballot and into office, but always keep in mind that new ground is often gained inch-by-inch.

One true story that illustrates this point comes from the life of one of our Founding Fathers, John Quincy Adams. Several Presidents of the United States also served in the House of Representatives before becoming President. But John Quincy Adams was the only one to serve in the House *after* serving as President. Can you imagine President Bush or President Clinton running for the House and serving as a freshman Member, being only one out of 435 Members after being THE Member at the other end of Pennsylvania Avenue?

Well, for John Quincy Adams the cause was far more important than the title. He arrived that first day and got right to work. Week after week, month after month, year after year, he brought legislation, petitions, and oral arguments condemning the practice of slavery and pleading for its abolition. He became known as the "hell hound of slavery." The problem was that he was bringing all of this before a very pro-slavery Congress. The pro-slavery members of Congress got so tired of his efforts that they passed a gag order preventing him from bringing anymore anti-slavery petitions to the floor.

After thirteen years of fighting this uphill battle, and by all appearances gaining absolutely no ground, a reporter asked him why he continued to fight. The reporter reminded him that he had seen no progress on the issue and wanted to know if he thought he was just wasting his time. John Quincy Adams responded with a statement that perfectly describes what our attitude should be in the political realm. He simply said,

## *"DUTY IS OURS, RESULTS ARE GOD'S"*

One year later, Congress lifted the gag order as the number of anti-slavery Members of Congress began to slowly increase. Did he see an end to slavery in his lifetime? No. He died on the floor of Congress after fighting a seventeen-year battle to end slavery, never seeing any real progress despite all his efforts.

But for one term while he was in Congress, John Quincy Adams became good friends with a freshman Member from Illinois. He mentored this young man and their friendship grew so much that the young man was a pallbearer at Adam's funeral.

The young man was never re-elected to another term in Congress and never won another election until 1860, when he was elected President of the United States. This young man, Abraham Lincoln, went on to implement virtually the same plan to abolish slavery that Adams had worked so long and hard to bring about. Finally, under Lincoln's watch, the principles of freedom embedded in the Declaration of Independence, and kept alive for seventeen years by the efforts of one man, were granted to all Americans.

My friends, we have no idea to whom we may be passing the torch, but God does. He has the plan. We just need to be faithful to do our part. He may be using our lives to plant seeds that others will one day come along and water. At times, we may get to see the fruits of our labor; at other times we may not. But regardless of the results, we have been given a sacred honor and trust as both Christians and Americans to be a light in a dark world. Our peace, though blessed when godly rulers are in office, ultimately does not come from our leaders in Washington: it comes from knowing that God truly is Sovereign and that He will take care of all the results.

# 24

# LET IT BEGIN HERE!

One of the greatest events in American history occurred on the morning of April 19, 1775, the morning following Paul Revere's ride. Seventy-seven minutemen assembled on that Lexington green. They were a small force of men and boys, black and white, literally a pastor and his parishioners. They did not look like much, but they stood strong in defense of freedom.

As those seventy-seven minutemen stood, six companies of British infantry approached. British Major Pitcairn rode up and shouted, *"Disperse ye rebels, disperse ye villains. Lay down your arms."*

Captain John Parker, captain of the minutemen, walked up and down the line of seventy-seven and said, *"Do not fire unless fired upon, but if they mean to have war, let it begin here!"*

Then the shot heard "round the world" was fired, and the fight for America's freedom was begun.

The minutemen lit the torch of freedom and passed it to the next generation, and for over two centuries, Americans have willingly accepted that torch and preserved it for their posterity. Now, it is our turn! This is our hour to stand guard at the watchtower of freedom. If that Torch of Freedom is to survive and be handed down from our generation to our children and grandchildren, then it has to begin *here!*

It begins on our knees, begging for God's mercy and grace on our nation. It begins in our churches, learning and applying a biblical worldview to every area of our lives, and then taking those truths to the world around us, becoming salt and light in our homes and communities.

Someday this chapter of history will be done. What will be said of the hour in which our generation stood guard? Will they say of us that it was on our watch the torch of freedom was extinguished? I pray not. My hope instead is that history's chapter on our generation will say that it was on our watch that the torch of freedom was lifted higher and burned brighter than ever before.

# APPENDIX A:
# A NOTE ABOUT TEACHING FREEDOM

*A nation which does not remember what it was yesterday, does not know what it is today, nor what it is trying to do. We are trying to do a futile thing if we don't know where we have come from, or what we have been about.*

**– President Woodrow Wilson**[99]

We can blame the school system all we want, but the truth is parents are the ones who are responsible for the education of our own children. Assuming we have a good relationship with our children, we can also influence the education of our grandchildren.

So, whether your child or grandchild is in public school, private school, or home school, get involved and bring history to life!

*Every child in America should be acquainted with his own country. He should read books that furnish him with ideas that will be useful to him in life and practice. As soon as he opens his lips, he should rehearse the history of his own country."*

**—Noah Webster**
*On the Education of Youth in America*
*1788*

One of the most exciting products on the market is "Drive Thru History," starring Dave Stott and produced by Focus on the Family. Dave Stott is so funny it keeps the kids engaged. David Barton consulted on the content, so you know you are getting accurate history. Your children will enjoy this entertaining program full of character building examples from history. To learn more about it, visit our website at www.wallbuilders.com.

Plan vacations with a purpose. When our children see the battlefield, or the museum, or The Freedom Trail, or the Lexington Green, or Independence Hall, it brings it to life and they rarely forget it. You can make it fun like our family does. They get to see a battlefield one day and a Major League Baseball game the next. Last year we saw the spot where George Washington was sworn in as president, then a Yankee game, and Mary Poppins on Broadway (to which my little girl exclaimed "finally, something besides a baseball game!"), and the Baseball Hall of Fame in Cooperstown. The point is you can bring history to life for your children without them feeling like they are sitting in a classroom.

If you do not have children or young grandchildren, plenty of opportunities still exist for you to pass the torch and instill these principles in the next generation. The best opportunity I can recommend is for you to sponsor a young person to attend Patriot Academy, for details go to, www.patriotacademy.com. This youth leadership program is training up the next generation of leaders with a biblical worldview of government, a firm grasp of the political process, and the skills necessary to WIN!

Our first responsibility is to those we are raising; then we should reach out to those in our churches and community. But we should not forget the vast majority of the youth of our nation still being educated in our public schools.

I have not given up on public education in this country. While choice and competition in education is the most important macro, overall change improves the product, I also believe in a couple of simple micro, or specific, changes that will improve our education system.

The Northwest Ordinance dealt with how new states were admitted into the union. This was one of the first laws passed under the new Constitution and signed by President Washington. The Founders required that each new state have an educational system, which taught three things in the following order: religion, morality, and knowledge.[100]

Today, we only teach knowledge—religion and morality have been removed from public schools. The Founders believed that knowledge alone was dangerous without religion and morality as a buffer. The French historian, Francois Guizot, asked James Russell Lowell, "How long will the American Republic endure?" Lowell replied, "As long as the ideas of the men who founded it continue to dominate."[101] Unfortunately, the ideas of our Founding Fathers are no longer dominant in this country and this change in educational emphasis is an obvious example.

Many people support the idea of getting the Bible or some form of moral absolutes into the public school classroom. While this can certainly be done constitutionally, just as our Founding Fathers did it, we will save that discussion for another day. For now, let me just suggest a way to inject moral absolutes, respect for life, and an acknowledgment of God back into our public education system without having to dance through the ridiculously complicated tests the Supreme Court has created in the last few decades.

The only source you need in the classroom to teach young people the basic, fundamental concepts of moral absolutes, respect for life, and the existence of God is...drum roll please...the founding documents of America. Right there in the Declaration and the Constitution, we find these principles in perhaps their most eloquent description. If we would just teach the actual language of these documents, we would see a difference in the culture within one generation.

When I served in the Texas Legislature, I proposed and the House passed House Bill 1776.[102] This legislation created "Celebrate Freedom Week" in public schools across Texas. During "Celebrate Freedom Week," children study the Founding Fathers and the Declaration of Independence, focusing on the following fifty-six words from the Declaration we studied earlier:

> *We hold these truths to be self-evident, that all men are created equal, that they are endowed by their Creator with certain unalienable Rights, that among these are Life, Liberty and the pursuit of Happiness. That to secure these rights, Governments are instituted among Men, deriving their just powers from the consent of the governed.*[103]

Despite the fact that we cannot teach from the Bible in the classroom, the biblical foundations of our government can be taught. Through these fifty-six words from the heart of the Declaration, we can instill in young people the knowledge that freedom and rights come from God. Therefore, there must be a Creator, and since freedom comes from Him, government cannot take that freedom away from the individual. The document makes it clear we are created beings and life is an unalienable right that must be protected. "Truths" worth fighting and dying for means moral relativism is wrong. Do you see the possibilities?

A court can interpret our founding documents however it wants, but if students read them and memorize them, they will get the foundation. They will know the truth, and will then be able to recognize the falsehood when courts misinterpret these documents.

Several states have modeled and passed legislation similar to House Bill 1776. You can help get it done in your state or you can make sure your local school district is participating.

When I first passed the law in the spring of 2001, an interesting thing happened. This was six months before 9/11 occurred and I was still getting those "American, so what?" looks and comments. In fact, when the education committee passed the bill out, the members on the committee took out little American flags and waived them in a mocking fashion because they thought I was being overly patriotic.

*Patriotism is as much a virtue as justice, and is as necessary for the support of societies as natural affection is for the support of families.*

**—Benjamin Rush**
*Letter to His Fellow Countrymen: On Patriotism, October 20, 1773*

Everyone thought the bill would pass with no problem. I had worked to gather more than one hundred democrat and republican co-authors who recognized the need for our children to better learn these basic concepts. The polling in our state showed that barely half of our citizens could name even one of the five freedoms in the First Amendment and only five percent could name two of those freedoms. If we do not know what our freedoms are, how will we know when they have been violated? How could we be willing to fight for them and defend them?

With more than two thirds of the House signing on, passage should have been a cinch, so the education committee sent the bill to the Local and Consent Calendar Committee, rather than the regular Calendars Committee. Both of these committees have the responsibility of setting the calendar for debate on the House Floor. The regular Calendars Committee is perhaps the most powerful committee in the Texas House because your bill never comes up for debate unless you get it through that committee and any member on that committee can tag your bill to prevent it from being set.

On the other hand, the Local and Consent Calendar is where a bill goes that only affects the author's district or is so non-controversial it will pass with ease, which is what the Education Committee expected with mine. But for some reason, my bill was not getting set on the Local and Consent Calendar to pass the House and go to the Senate. I finally found out that a member of the committee had a problem with the bill and was holding it up, so I went to visit with him. It turns out he did not like the provision that had children recite the fifty-six words from the heart of the Declaration, even though I had an "opt out clause" where a student's parents could opt them out of this activity during Celebrate Freedom Week if they had some reason of conscience to do so.

This state representative, for reasons I still do not understand to this day, exploded with rage telling me *"you have no right to tell these kids to repeat those things."* His attitude and comments reflected exactly those of the Ninth Circuit in *Newdow v. Congress*. Once again, the idea of our education system actually taking a position on worldview and instilling the basic strategies of our national success was an abhorrent idea to some. I would have expected this from a left wing democrat, but this guy was a Republican from a conservative district.

Well, the good news is that we finally got the bill passed, although I was forced by this certain state representative to change the wording in the bill from "required" to "permissive". This means that a school district could do it or not do it, and it was up to local citizens to make them do it. A lot of citizens did so and I always enjoyed the letters and pictures children would send me from their participation in Celebrate Freedom Week at their local school.

In 2003, my friend, Representative Bryan Hughes, modified the statute back to the way I had originally written it so that every school is now required to participate. But laws like this are difficult to enforce, so if you live in Texas, you can help teach freedom by simply raising the issue with your local school board and find out if they are implementing a Celebrate Freedom Week.

About a dozen other states have now passed similar legislation. If your state has not done so, go visit with your legislators and ask them to join you in the effort to teach freedom.

*Let the American youth never forget, that they possess a noble inheritance, bought by the toils, and sufferings, and blood of their ancestors; and capacity, if wisely improved, and faithfully guarded, of transmitting to their latest posterity all the substantial blessings of life, the peaceful enjoyment of liberty, property, religion, and independence.*

—**Joseph Story**
*Commentaries on the Constitution*
*1833*

# APPENDIX B:
# WHERE DO WE GO FROM HERE?

A Warning to the Republican Party
(Speech Delivered By Rick Green February 4, 2006
To Hays County Lincoln Day Dinner)

If you remember anything I say tonight, I pray it is this: Just as in the famous Reagan speech of 1964, it is again a time for choosing. We Republicans have had a season of harvest in terms of elections and some victories in terms of policy, but the major policy challenges of our day are yet to be addressed and the battle is far, far from over.

The choice before us is clear: will we choose to become fat and lazy on the comfort and spoils of campaign victories or will we charge ahead to enjoy the history making results of real change?

Our greatest threat comes not from our opposition, but from among our own. We are at great risk of not only losing steam, but also completely missing the historical opportunities of our generation because too many among us value our own re-election more than actually accomplishing the agenda for which we were first elected.

If we allow ourselves to become like the big government elitists we defeated, the voters will throw out the republicans and the major goals of the conservative revolution will fade away. **We must clarify our mission, hold our leaders accountable, and prepare the next generation to continue the revolution.**

Most everyone in this room has heard me speak. You know that I'm not a "doom and gloomer." I travel the nation giving what I pray are inspirational messages of hope for our future and do my best to leave an audience feeling good, but also ready to take action. My speeches are usually full of jokes, as well as emotional stories and in my dreams, folks are laughing one minute and crying the next... but it doesn't always work out that way.

Well, this is not one of those speeches. Partly because this audience knows all of my jokes and most of my stories... but mostly because there is a season for everything. I have to admit that I just don't feel like this is the time for jokes or feel good anecdotes. Rather, I believe this is the time for a real hard look at who we are and where we are going as a political party.

I stood before you six years ago at this same event and said *"It's no longer a question of whether or not republicans will be in charge. The question is what KIND of republicans will lead, what kind of leadership will we provide, and what kind of legacy will we leave."*

Well, tonight, I consider you family and so I will speak to you as family, with all candor—respectful, but truthful. The way Patrick Henry started his famous *"Give me liberty or give me death"* speech on March 23, 1775, applies here: *"in proportion to the magnitude of the subject ought to be the freedom of the debate. It is only in this way that we can hope to arrive at the truth, and fulfill the great responsibility which we hold to God and our country. Should I keep back my opinions at such a time, through fear of giving offense, I should consider myself as guilty of treason towards my country, and of an act of disloyalty toward the Majesty of Heaven, which I revere above all earthly kings."* In my language of country boy speak, that just means the stakes are too high to mince words out of fear that I might offend someone. So hold back, I will not.

Here we are six years later. We Republicans have gotten really good at winning elections. Nationally we hold the White House and both Houses of Congress, we now hold majorities in more state legislative bodies than the D's, a strong majority of Governors are republican, and right here in Texas we have the Governor's mansion, the senate, a HUGE majority in the Texas House, and every single Statewide elective office.

It was not always this way. Many of you in this room remember when it was, in fact, exactly the opposite. Barely two decades ago democrats held all of these offices and enjoyed comfortable majorities. But as their party moved further to the left, they lost more and more favor with the true conservative majority of this state and nation.

As they weakened, we became more aggressive. A generation of conservatives were inspired by Ronald Reagan, educated and motivated by Rush Limbaugh and David Barton, and then little by little we started taking ground (clawing our way through every inch) until we now hold the lever on virtually every source of power in the nation, but to what end?

What has been the fruit of our labor? Do you remember when you first got inspired enough to take action? What was the issue, what was the cause? What was it that you wanted to see changed so bad that it inspired you to give of your time, your money, your energy to help get good people elected and change public policy. Can you remember a specific issue? Has it changed? Did we win? Is it better?

On many things it certainly is. We defeated communism, outlawed partial birth abortion, and many other victories, some small and some large.

But how do we measure up lately? When I first got involved in politics in the late 1980's, getting rid of the federal department of education was a top conservative goal. Republicans have now made it larger than democrats ever even tried. When I was elected to the Texas House, we republicans derided the democrats for growing the budget at ten percent. Our comfortable republican majorities just gave us a twenty-one percent increase in the budget!

On the local level, even our republicans have hidden behind out of control property value increases to spend like the democrats, but claim they didn't raise taxes. Everyone says the other guy is using fuzzy math. Well, I just automatically assume I'm not smart enough to work through all their figures, so I just look at the bottom line. Is my property tax bill bigger or smaller than it was under the democrats?

Friends, there's not a person in this room that is paying less, we're all paying more—more in local taxes, more in state taxes, more in federal taxes, and all of it has been given to us by republicans.

Now, aren't you glad you came to this meeting to get depressed?

Lest you think that I've given up on the Republican Party, let me stop for a second and give some of the successes. Thanks to President Bush's uncompromising fight on terror, the terrorists have not had another successful attack on our homeland since 9/11. Every one of us expected additional attacks within weeks, yet five years later, there has not been a successful one and the credit belongs to republicans who have stood their ground and rejected the John Kerry approach of appeasement.

Right here in Texas, we have ushered through tort reform, parental consent for an abortion, defense of marriage, and in the first republican session of 2003, we actually held the line on spending because of a super Texas republican named Talmadge Heflin. None of those things would have happened under the democrats, so we've had a few victories and should be proud of them.

But now what? Where do we go from here?

What about the major issues of school finance, property taxes, education choice, out of control entitlement spending, loss of property rights, run away courts, and continued attacks on our religious liberties?

We have been very aggressive on the campaign trail, but once in office, our leaders are timid on the major policy issues of our day. We win the election, and then leave government much the same as it was under those we defeated. Why? Why are we so afraid to enact the very things that were obviously popular enough with the people to get us elected in the first place?

Is the beast so big that it truly cannot be tamed? I don't believe that for a minute. Let me give you a non-American example. My young friend Torsten Pederson is a freshman member of the Danish Parliament and even as a freshman he has passed legislation to completely restructure and shrink what has become a socialistic system. If they can do it in Denmark, we can do it here!

Or is power so corrupting that even the well-intentioned leaders we worked so hard for, now care more about keeping their power than doing the job for which we elected them?

I have always been against term limits, even when the democrats were in power and it looked impossible for us to overcome the power of their incumbency, but now that I've seen our folks seem to buy into the *"I have to get re-elected before I can change things"* mentality, I'm starting to reconsider the idea. The main reason I'm starting to re-consider it is because the smartest women in the world, no, it's not Hillary Clinton, it's Kara Green, is trying to convince me. But I'm still against them because I'd rather us just elect good folks like US. Senator Tom Coburn from Oklahoma who says he'll only serve two terms and he does not care if he is not re-elected for the second term. He's immediately moving aggressively forward with the conservative agenda for which he was elected. We need more like him, especially here in Texas.

Here we are, basking in the success of our election victories. Victories that all of us in this room worked for years to bring about, but we weren't giving of our blood, sweat and tears just so that a "party" would be in control, we worked so that a philosophy would be put in place and public policy would change. So now that our party is in control but the major policy items are stalled, what should we do?

Where DO we go from here? Well, first, we don't abandon the party or the process.

When Harriet Miers was nominated for the U.S. Supreme Court last fall, I got all kinds of calls from people saying that was the final straw and they were checking out of the process. They were tired of working so hard to be rewarded this way. Folks, we're going to have our peaks and our valleys, our seasons of harvest and seasons of famine, victories and defeats, but we don't cut and run; only democrats do that when they run to Ardmore and New Mexico![ii] We stay the course; we continue to fight the fight and never lose heart. Nobody ever said it would be easy, but they did say it would be worth it and I still believe that with all my heart. The Miers nomination is a great case in point. Conservatives stayed in the fight, held President Bush accountable and the nomination was withdrawn and was replaced with a very solid conservative for the highest court.

Freedom is not only worth dying for, it's worth living and fighting for. Patrick Henry went on in that same speech to say *"If we wish to be free--if we mean to preserve inviolate those inestimable privileges for which we have been so long contending—if we mean not basely to abandon the noble struggle in which we have been so long engaged, and which we have pledged ourselves never to abandon until the glorious object of our contest shall be obtained—we must fight!"*

Henry was staring in the face of the most powerful military in the world and calling men to fight with bullets and war. I am simply charging you tonight to fight with ballots in a war of words to preserve the purpose of this party and make our philosophy into policy.

We must decide now how we will fight and which battles are most important. At this time for choosing, here's my two cents on specific steps we can take over the next few years to usher in a new wave of conservatism and reignite the Reagan revolution.

---

[ii] For those readers outside of Texas, this was a reference to Texas democrat legislators literally running away and hiding out in another state to keep the Legislature from doing its work…simply because they were in the minority and could not get their way. It was a toddler response that embarrassed Texas and every single one of the cowards should have been fired by their constituents.

Now, if you're one of those country club, finger to the wind, want to be popular more than you want to be a patriot kind of republicans - you folks probably ought to leave right now 'cause I'd rather you not know our winning strategy. Go ahead, we'll wait for you to pack up your things.

## Five steps that I suggest:

**First**, we stick with the party and work from within for as long as it's the most viable option for enacting a conservative, founding father's philosophy, which I believe will be the case for most of our lifetimes at least. Do not get distracted by these third party movements that only weaken us, stick with the party! That doesn't mean we'll always be in power, the pendulum swings and there will always be seasons of planting and seasons of harvest, but it means we don't cut and run in the tough times.

It makes absolutely no strategic sense to walk away from a powerful party structure where conservatives have more than half the ranks, to go start from scratch and try to build an equally large and powerful apparatus. The smart move is to stay focused and mobilized within the Republican Party and nominate better candidates out of the primary.

**Second**, we avoid extremism that labels an entire profession or group of people as evil. Such small mindedness and short sightedness will diminish us and destroy us. I do not speak of religious labels or categories, but to the absolute, no questions asked, lock stock and barrel sellout by republicans to insurance companies and the business lobby on the issue of tort reform.

Now before you say that I sound like a democrat, take a hard look at who is talking here. I helped pass and supported every tort reform measure of my four years in the legislature and supported the measures before and after that period. There is no question that the tobacco trial lawyers and many plaintiff lawyers have abused our system to their own gain and ran businesses out of Texas. We have passed many very, very good measures to correct much of the problem.

But in the process, we have become the very thing we accused the democrats of for years. We accurately said they were sold out to trial lawyers, bought and paid for by contributions, and we watched them do whatever the trial lawyers wanted, whether it was blocking common sense reforms or making those same lawyers rich through the tobacco litigation scandals.

Well, look at how republicans now react to the tort reform lobby. When they say jump, too many in our party say "how high?" We pass any legislation the lawsuit reform groups want, even when it goes too far and slams the door on the little guy. We label anyone with a law degree that steps into a courtroom as an evil trial lawyer, no matter what other good they may do in their personal lives in their family, churches, community, or even the good they do in the courtroom or other public policy battles.

Well friends, I have defended those who could not defend themselves, I have filed lawsuits in order to right wrongs. Does that make me an evil trial lawyer? I could say the same of John Adams, Daniel Webster, John Quincy Adams, and so many others.

There are honorable men and women of the legal profession that are with us on virtually every issue from stopping the murder of abortion to ending the theft by taxes system we call school finance and a million other issues in between. But simply because they practice law, we shut them out, refuse their contributions, and allow our fellow republicans to call even the good ones sharks and every other name in the book. It's wrong and in terms of a strategy for building winning coalitions, it's shortsighted and just plain stupid.

Oh and by the way, on the flip side, not only do we shut out an entire group of people because of this one issue, but we also have republicans putting their arms around liberal democrats because of this one issue. (Democrat State Representative) Patrick

Rose is the darling of the tort reformers, so when republican leaders are told by the tort reformers to protect him do they think about the fact that he votes against every education reform, against every plan to cut property taxes, against every piece of pro-life or school choice legislation? No, these republicans simply say "how high?" We have the best candidate for State Representative that Hays County has seen in at least twenty years. A man who has served us honorably in battle, given twenty years of service to us in the military, served our community and schools, solved school finance locally and is the perfect guy to go to Austin to help solve it, a businessman and a family man. But we have the republican speaker of the house posing for pictures with the democrat incumbent. You think he's doing that because he thinks a 25 year old who has never even had a real job will be a better rep than Jim Neuhaus? No, he's doing it to try and protect his own job as Speaker because it's what some of the big contributors want. It's an embarrassment to our party and we need leaders who have the courage to say no to the big contributors when they are wrong! Let's start by doing everything within our means to prove the sold out establishment wrong and elect Jim Neuhaus to the Legislature.

**Third**, we must set very specific, inspiring, and worthy goals that will motivate a new generation of conservatives to join the fight and keep the current generation engaged. I don't pretend to be smart enough to set those goals by myself, but just to get the conversation rolling, I'll throw out a few ideas. If one were making a list of the four or five most important issues to preserving freedom for the next generation, I would think they had to include:

1. Winning the war on terror.
2. Child Centered Funding. Until we put parents back in charge of their children's education and give them choice, then the system of education will not improve. We should make it an absolute must before we support a candidate for the legislature.
3. Reigning in the federal courts: We need to challenge Congress to do their duty and reign in the courts. The

Constitution clearly gives them the power to limit the jurisdiction of the courts, abolish courts that go too far, and impeach judges who seem to think they are legislators. The Founders made it clear the court was to be the weakest branch, but we have allowed it to become the strongest because Congress is not doing its job and using the checks and balances given to it by the people. We should also consider a Constitutional Amendment to define the term of federal judges. I don't even care what the term is to be. Six years? Ten, maybe even fifteen? The point is the Founders did not intend them to be appointed for life. The Constitution says they are appointed for "good behavior" which today seems to mean they have a pulse. Setting a defined term would hold them more directly accountable at some point if they want to be re-appointed. It would also reduce the circus surrounding a Supreme Court nomination because it becomes less important since that Justice is not being given three or four decades to impact the nation. It would take a lot of work to accomplish this amendment, but it is worth considering.

4. <u>We must end the holocaust of abortion and return to a culture of life.</u> Though controversial, this is not complicated. Either it is life or it is not. Anyone viewing the 4D sonogram images now available cannot possible say it is not life. As a life, that baby has unalienable rights and deserves our protection. Our nation is paying a dear price for thirty years of infanticide, literally sacrificing our children on the altar of convenience.

5. <u>Immigration.</u> I don't pretend to know the answer and I hope someone in this room smarter than me will come up with one. But I know we must secure our borders and we must know who the guest workers are and where they are. It seems to me we should make it a thousand times harder to get into our country illegally, but also make it a thousand times easier to get into our country LEGALLY because we need the guest workers.

**Fourth**, we must recruit, train, and work for candidates that are leaders of true conviction, willing to take on tough fights. That means we run like crazy from the politicians that just want to be somebody and have a fancy title. Since we became the party of power, we have become infested with these self-absorbed, egotistical empty suits.

So let's clean house from within, support reformers that are well grounded and have a sense of specific purpose, not just a desire to be on the ballot. This also means that we don't discourage opposition in the primary. How dare we take on the democrat's attitude that ANY of our leaders are "entitled" to the position and should not be challenged, especially when there is a true difference between the incumbent and the challenger.

Besides, if our incumbent is doing the right things and deserves to be re-elected, they will be stronger because of the challenge. However, the loser of that primary has a duty and responsibility to go to the winner and make peace, lock arms and work together towards victory in the fall, with rare exceptions. Part of the reason a democrat now represents us in the Legislature is that the moderate republicans who opposed me in the primary refused our efforts to join forces and some of them even helped the democrat. So, incumbents and challengers, you guys owe it to every republican activist in this room and across this county to do your best to win on March 7th, but if you wake on March 8th and you are not the victor, be the first to join the other team and take us to victory in November. We are counting on you guys higher up the ballot to set the example for all of the races down ballot from you.

**Fifth**, we must build a farm team by preparing the next generation. I urge you to join me in supporting Patriot Academy. This program is raising up a well-prepared generation of conservative leaders who truly get it. They understand the times and they know what to do. They are intelligent, passionate, articulate, and the future looks bright every time I have the pleasure of watching them debate on the House Floor. The Torch of Freedom is not a self-sustaining flame; it must be stoked and guarded by each generation. You and I have a responsibility to prepare the next generation for receiving that Torch at the time we pass it on to them.

Let me close tonight by speaking to the more elderly members of our family here with us. You are not done giving and doing for this party and nation until your body is six feet under and your soul is in heaven. We need you, your counsel, your wisdom, and your action. As we are training up the next generation to accept the Torch of Freedom, who better to teach them how to protect it than those who are actually passing it. We all have a role to play and yours is nowhere near done.

Russell Kirk said "Politics is the art of the possible." Let's never be the ones to say it can't be done, let us be believers in the possible, we've done what no one thought we could in terms of winning elections, now let's do our part to make sure that the power we have accumulated is not the end game, just power for the sake of power. Let's make sure it is power with a purpose. Let's write a chapter in history that says when we were in charge, the torch burned brighter than ever before.

*(Nine months after this speech was delivered, Republicans would lose their majority in Congress, lose seats in the Texas House, and lose three of their four seats on the Hays County Commissioner's Court, Rick's home County where the speech was given.)*

# Appendix C:
# Slavery and the Founding Fathers
# by David Barton

Even though the issue of slavery is often raised as a discrediting charge against the Founding Fathers, the historical fact is that slavery was not the product of, nor was it an evil introduced by, the Founding Fathers; slavery had been introduced to America nearly two centuries before the Founders. As President of Congress Henry Laurens explained:

> *I abhor slavery. I was born in a country where slavery had been established by British Kings and Parliaments as well as by the laws of the country ages before my existence. . . . In former days there was no combating the prejudices of men supported by interest; the day, I hope, is approaching when, from principles of gratitude as well as justice, every man will strive to be foremost in showing his readiness to comply with the Golden Rule ["do unto others as you would have them do unto you" Matthew 7:12].* [1]

Prior to the time of the Founding Fathers, there had been few serious efforts to dismantle the institution of slavery. John Jay identified the point at which the change in attitude toward slavery began:

> *Prior to the great Revolution, the great majority . . . of our people had been so long accustomed to the practice and convenience of having slaves that very few among them even doubted the propriety and rectitude of it.* [2]

The Revolution was the turning point in the national attitude—and it was the Founding Fathers who contributed greatly to that change. In fact, many of the Founders vigorously complained against the fact that Great Britain had forcefully imposed upon the Colonies the evil of slavery. For example, Thomas Jefferson heavily criticized that British policy:

> He [King George III] has waged cruel war against human nature itself, violating its most sacred rights of life and liberty in the persons of a distant people who never offended him, captivating and carrying them into slavery in another hemisphere or to incur miserable death in their transportation thither. . . . Determined to keep open a market where men should be bought and sold, he has prostituted his negative for suppressing every legislative attempt to prohibit or to restrain this execrable commerce [that is, he has opposed efforts to prohibit the slave trade]. [3]

Benjamin Franklin, in a 1773 letter to Dean Woodward, confirmed that whenever the Americans had attempted to end slavery, the British government had indeed thwarted those attempts. Franklin explained that . . .

> . . . a disposition to abolish slavery prevails in North America, that many of Pennsylvanians have set their slaves at liberty, and that even the Virginia Assembly have petitioned the King for permission to make a law for preventing the importation of more into that colony. This request, however, will probably not be granted as their former laws of that kind have always been repealed. [4]

Further confirmation that even the Virginia Founders were not responsible for slavery, but actually tried to dismantle the institution, was provided by John Quincy Adams (known as the "hell-hound of abolition" for his extensive efforts against that evil). Adams explained:

> The inconsistency of the institution of domestic slavery with the principles of the Declaration of Independence was seen and lamented by all the southern patriots of the Revolution; by no one with deeper and more unalterable conviction than by the author of the Declaration himself [Jefferson]. No charge of insincerity or hypocrisy can be fairly laid to their charge. Never from their lips

*was heard one syllable of attempt to justify the institution of slavery. They universally considered it as a reproach fastened upon them by the unnatural step-mother country [Great Britain] and they saw that before the principles of the Declaration of Independence, slavery, in common with every other mode of oppression, was destined sooner or later to be banished from the earth. Such was the undoubting conviction of Jefferson to his dying day. In the Memoir of His Life, written at the age of seventy-seven, he gave to his countrymen the solemn and emphatic warning that the day was not distant when they must hear and adopt the general emancipation of their slaves.* [5]

While Jefferson himself had introduced a bill designed to end slavery, [6] not all of the southern Founders were opposed to slavery. According to the testimony of Virginians James Madison, Thomas Jefferson, and John Rutledge, it was the Founders from North Carolina, South Carolina, and Georgia who most strongly favored slavery. [7] Yet, despite the support for slavery in those States, the clear majority of the Founders opposed this evil. For instance, when some of the southern pro-slavery advocates invoked the Bible in support of slavery, Elias Boudinot, President of the Continental Congress, responded:

*[E]ven the sacred Scriptures had been quoted to justify this iniquitous traffic. It is true that the Egyptians held the Israelites in bondage for four hundred years, . . . but . . . gentlemen cannot forget the consequences that followed: they were delivered by a strong hand and stretched-out arm and it ought to be remembered that the Almighty Power that accomplished their deliverance is the same yesterday, today, and for ever.* [8]

Many of the Founding Fathers who had owned slaves as British citizens released them in the years following America's separation from Great Britain (e.g., George Washington, John Dickinson, Caesar Rodney, William Livingston, George Wythe, John Randolph of Roanoke, and others). Furthermore, many of the Founders had never owned any slaves. For example, John Adams proclaimed, "[M]y opinion against it [slavery] has always been known . . . [N]ever in my life did I own a slave."[9]

Notice a few additional examples of the strong anti-slavery sentiments held by great numbers of the Founders:

*[W]hy keep alive the question of slavery? It is admitted by all to be a great evil.* [10]

## CHARLES CARROLL, SIGNER OF THE DECLARATION

*As Congress is now to legislate for our extensive territory lately acquired, I pray to Heaven that they may build up the system of the government on the broad, strong, and sound principles of freedom. Curse not the inhabitants of those regions, and of the United States in general, with a permission to introduce bondage [slavery].* [11]

## JOHN DICKINSON, SIGNER OF THE CONSTITUTION; GOVERNOR OF PENNSYLVANIA

*That men should pray and fight for their own freedom and yet keep others in slavery is certainly acting a very inconsistent, as well as unjust and perhaps impious, part.* [12]

## JOHN JAY, PRESIDENT OF CONTINENTAL CONGRESS, ORIGINAL CHIEF JUSTICE U. S. SUPREME COURT

*The whole commerce between master and slave is a perpetual exercise of the most boisterous passions, the most unremitting despotism on the one part, and degrading submissions on the other...And with what execration [curse] should the statesman be loaded, who permitting one half the citizens thus to trample on the rights of the other. . . . And can the liberties of a nation be thought secure when we have removed their only firm basis, a conviction in the minds of the people that these liberties are of the gift of God?*

*That they are not to be violated but with His wrath? Indeed I tremble for my country when I reflect that God is just; that his justice cannot sleep forever.* [13]

## THOMAS JEFFERSON

*Christianity, by introducing into Europe the truest principles of humanity, universal benevolence, and brotherly love, had happily abolished civil slavery. Let us who profess the same religion practice its precepts . . . by agreeing to this duty.* [14]

## RICHARD HENRY LEE, PRESIDENT OF CONTINENTAL CONGRESS; SIGNER OF THE DECLARATION

*I hope we shall at last, and if it so please God I hope it may be during my life time, see this cursed thing [slavery] taken out. . . . For my part, whether in a public station or a private capacity, I shall always be prompt to contribute my assistance towards effecting so desirable an event.* [15]

## WILLIAM LIVINGSTON, SIGNER OF THE CONSTITUTION; GOVERNOR OF NEW JERSEY

*[I]t ought to be considered that national crimes can only be and frequently are punished in this world by national punishments; and that the continuance of the slave-trade, and thus giving it a national sanction and encouragement, ought to be considered as justly exposing us to the displeasure and vengeance of Him who is equally Lord of all and who views with equal eye the poor African slave and his American master.* [16]

## LUTHER MARTIN, DELEGATE AT CONSTITUTIONAL CONVENTION

*As much as I value a union of all the States, I would not admit the Southern States into the Union unless they agree to the discontinuance of this disgraceful trade [slavery].* [17]

*Honored will that State be in the annals of history which shall first abolish this violation of the rights of mankind.* [18]

JOSEPH REED, REVOLUTIONARY OFFICER;
GOVERNOR OF PENNSYLVANIA

*Domestic slavery is repugnant to the principles of Christianity. . . . It is rebellion against the authority of a common Father. It is a practical denial of the extent and efficacy of the death of a common Savior. It is an usurpation of the prerogative of the great Sovereign of the universe who has solemnly claimed an exclusive property in the souls of men.* [19]

BENJAMIN RUSH, SIGNER OF THE
DECLARATION

*Justice and humanity require it [the end of slavery]—Christianity commands it. Let every benevolent . . . pray for the glorious period when the last slave who fights for freedom shall be restored to the possession of that inestimable right.* [20]

NOAH WEBSTER, RESPONSIBLE FOR ARTICLE I,
SECTION 8, ¶ 8 OF THE CONSTITUTION

*Slavery, or an absolute and unlimited power in the master over the life and fortune of the slave, is unauthorized by the common law. . . . The reasons which we sometimes see assigned for the origin and the continuance of slavery appear, when examined to the bottom, to be built upon a false foundation. In the enjoyment of their persons and of their property, the common law protects all.* [21]

JAMES WILSON, SIGNER OF THE
CONSTITUTION;

U. S. SUPREME COURT JUSTICE

*[I]t is certainly unlawful to make inroads upon others . . . and take away their liberty by no better means than superior power.* [22]

## JOHN WITHERSPOON, SIGNER OF THE DECLARATION

For many of the Founders, their feelings against slavery went beyond words. For example, in 1774, Benjamin Franklin and Benjamin Rush founded America's first anti-slavery society; John Jay was president of a similar society in New York. In fact, when signer of the Constitution William Livingston heard of the New York society, he, as Governor of New Jersey, wrote them, offering:

I would most ardently wish to become a member of it [the society in New York] and . . . I can safely promise them that neither my tongue, nor my pen, nor purse shall be wanting to promote the abolition of what to me appears so inconsistent with humanity and Christianity. . . . May the great and the equal Father of the human race, who has expressly declared His abhorrence of oppression, and that He is no respecter of persons, succeed a design so laudably calculated to undo the heavy burdens, to let the oppressed go free, and to break every yoke. [23]

Other prominent Founding Fathers who were members of societies for ending slavery included Richard Bassett, James Madison, James Monroe, Bushrod Washington, Charles Carroll, William Few, John Marshall, Richard Stockton, Zephaniah Swift, and many more. In fact, based in part on the efforts of these Founders, Pennsylvania and Massachusetts began abolishing slavery in 1780; [24] Connecticut and Rhode Island did so in 1784; [25] Vermont in 1786; [26] New Hampshire in 1792; [27] New York in 1799; [28] and New Jersey did so in 1804. [29]

Additionally, the reason that Ohio, Indiana, Illinois, Michigan, Wisconsin, and Iowa all prohibited slavery was a Congressional act, authored by Constitution signer Rufus King [30] and signed into law by President George Washington, [31] which prohibited slavery in those territories. [32] It is not surprising that Washington would sign such a law, for it was he who had declared:

> I can only say that there is not a man living who wishes more sincerely than I do to see a plan adopted for the abolition of it [slavery]. [33]

The truth is that it was the Founding Fathers who were responsible for planting and nurturing the first seeds for the recognition of black equality and for the eventual end of slavery. This was a fact made clear by Richard Allen.

Allen had been a slave in Pennsylvania but was freed after he converted his master to Christianity. Allen, a close friend of Benjamin Rush and several other Founding Fathers, went on to become the founder of the A.M.E. Church in America. In an early address "To the People of Color," he explained:

> Many of the white people have been instruments in the hands of God for our good, even such as have held us in captivity, [and] are now pleading our cause with earnestness and zeal. [34]

While much progress was made by the Founders to end the institution of slavery, unfortunately what they began was not fully achieved until generations later. Yet, despite the strenuous effort of many Founders to recognize in practice that "all men are created equal," charges persist to the opposite. In fact, revisionists even claim that the Constitution demonstrates that the Founders considered one who was black to be only three-fifths of a person. This charge is yet another falsehood. The three-fifths clause was not a measurement of human worth; rather, it was an anti-slavery provision to limit the political power of slavery's proponents. By including only three-fifths of the total number of slaves in the congressional calculations, Southern States were actually being denied additional pro-slavery representatives in Congress. Based on the clear records of the Constitutional Convention, two prominent professors explain the meaning of the three-fifths clause:

[T]he Constitution allowed Southern States to count three-fifths of their slaves toward the population that would determine numbers of representatives in the federal legislature. This clause is often singled out today as a sign of black dehumanization: they are only three-fifths human. But the provision applied to slaves, not blacks. That meant that free blacks–and there were many, North as well as South–counted the same as whites. More important, the fact that slaves were counted at all was a concession to slave owners. Southerners would have been glad to count their slaves as whole persons. It was the Northerners who did not want them counted, for why should the South be rewarded with more representatives, the more slaves they held? [35] THOMAS WEST

It was slavery's opponents who succeeded in restricting the political power of the South by allowing them to count only three-fifths of their slave population in determining the number of congressional representatives. The three-fifths of a vote provision applied only to slaves, not to free blacks in either the North or South. [36] WALTER WILLIAMS

Why do revisionists so often abuse and misportray the three-fifths clause? Professor Walter Williams (himself an African-American) suggested:

Politicians, news media, college professors and leftists of other stripes are selling us lies and propaganda. To lay the groundwork for their increasingly successful attack on our Constitution, they must demean and criticize its authors. As Senator Joe Biden demonstrated during the Clarence Thomas hearings, the framers' ideas about natural law must be trivialized or they must be seen as racists. [37]

While this has been only a cursory examination of the Founders and slavery, it is nonetheless sufficient to demonstrate the absurdity of the insinuation that the Founders were a collective group of racists.

For more information on this issue see *George Washington, Thomas Jefferson & Slavery in Virginia, The Bible, Slavery, and America's Founders, Black History Issue 2003, Confronting Civil War Revisionism,* and *Setting the Record Straight* (Book, DVD, or VHS) all at www.wallbuilders.com.

# Appendix D:
# The Declaration of Independence

IN CONGRESS, July 4, 1776.

The unanimous Declaration of the thirteen united States of America,

When in the Course of human events, it becomes necessary for one people to dissolve the political bands which have connected them with another, and to assume among the powers of the earth, the separate and equal station to which the Laws of Nature and of Nature's God entitle them, a decent respect to the opinions of mankind requires that they should declare the causes which impel them to the separation.

We hold these truths to be self-evident, that all men are created equal, that they are endowed by their Creator with certain unalienable Rights, that among these are Life, Liberty and the pursuit of Happiness. --That to secure these rights, Governments are instituted among Men, deriving their just powers from the consent of the governed, -- That whenever any Form of Government becomes destructive of these ends, it is the Right of the People to alter or to abolish it, and to institute new Government, laying its foundation on such principles and organizing its powers in such form, as to them shall seem most likely to effect their Safety and Happiness. Prudence, indeed, will dictate that Governments long established should not be changed for light and transient causes; and accordingly all experience hath shewn, that mankind are more disposed to suffer, while evils are sufferable, than to right themselves by abolishing the forms to which they are accustomed. But when a long train of abuses and usurpations, pursuing invariably the same Object evinces a design to reduce them under absolute Despotism, it is their right, it is their duty, to throw off such Government, and to provide new Guards for their future security.--Such has been the patient sufferance of these Colonies; and such is now the necessity which constrains them to alter their former Systems of Government. The history of the present King of Great Britain is a history of repeated injuries and usurpations, all having in direct object the establishment of an absolute Tyranny over these States. To prove this, let Facts be submitted to a candid world.

He has refused his Assent to Laws, the most wholesome and necessary for the public good.

He has forbidden his Governors to pass Laws of immediate and pressing importance, unless suspended in their operation till his Assent should be obtained; and when so suspended, he has utterly neglected to attend to them.

He has refused to pass other Laws for the accommodation of large districts of people, unless those people would relinquish the right of Representation in the Legislature, a right inestimable to them and formidable to tyrants only.

He has called together legislative bodies at places unusual, uncomfortable, and distant from the depository of their public Records, for the sole purpose of fatiguing them into compliance with his measures.

He has dissolved Representative Houses repeatedly, for opposing with manly firmness his invasions on the rights of the people.

He has refused for a long time, after such dissolutions, to cause others to be elected; whereby the Legislative powers, incapable of Annihilation, have returned to the People at large for their exercise; the State remaining in the mean time exposed to all the dangers of invasion from without, and convulsions within.

He has endeavoured to prevent the population of these States; for that purpose obstructing the Laws for Naturalization of Foreigners; refusing to pass others to encourage their migrations hither, and raising the conditions of new Appropriations of Lands.

He has obstructed the Administration of Justice, by refusing his Assent to Laws for establishing Judiciary powers.

He has made Judges dependent on his Will alone, for the tenure of their offices, and the amount and payment of their salaries.

He has erected a multitude of New Offices, and sent hither swarms of Officers to harrass our people, and eat out their substance.

He has kept among us, in times of peace, Standing Armies without the Consent of our legislatures.

He has affected to render the Military independent of and superior to the Civil power.

He has combined with others to subject us to a jurisdiction foreign to our constitution, and unacknowledged by our laws; giving his Assent to their Acts of pretended Legislation:

For Quartering large bodies of armed troops among us:

For protecting them, by a mock Trial, from punishment for any Murders which they should commit on the Inhabitants of these States:

For cutting off our Trade with all parts of the world:

For imposing Taxes on us without our Consent:

For depriving us in many cases, of the benefits of Trial by Jury:

For transporting us beyond Seas to be tried for pretended offences

For abolishing the free System of English Laws in a neighbouring Province, establishing therein an Arbitrary government, and enlarging its

Boundaries so as to render it at once an example and fit instrument for introducing the same absolute rule into these Colonies:

For taking away our Charters, abolishing our most valuable Laws, and altering fundamentally the Forms of our Governments:

For suspending our own Legislatures, and declaring themselves invested with power to legislate for us in all cases whatsoever.

He has abdicated Government here, by declaring us out of his Protection and waging War against us.

He has plundered our seas, ravaged our Coasts, burnt our towns, and destroyed the lives of our people.

He is at this time transporting large Armies of foreign Mercenaries to compleat the works of death, desolation and tyranny, already begun with circumstances of Cruelty & perfidy scarcely paralleled in the most barbarous ages, and totally unworthy the Head of a civilized nation.

He has constrained our fellow Citizens taken Captive on the high Seas to bear Arms against their Country, to become the executioners of their friends and Brethren, or to fall themselves by their Hands.

He has excited domestic insurrections amongst us, and has endeavoured to bring on the inhabitants of our frontiers, the merciless Indian Savages, whose known rule of warfare, is an undistinguished destruction of all ages, sexes and conditions.

In every stage of these Oppressions We have Petitioned for Redress in the most humble terms: Our repeated Petitions have been answered only by repeated injury. A Prince whose character is thus marked by every act which may define a Tyrant, is unfit to be the ruler of a free people.

Nor have We been wanting in attentions to our Brittish brethren. We have warned them from time to time of attempts by their legislature to extend an unwarrantable jurisdiction over us. We have reminded them of the circumstances of our emigration and settlement here. We have appealed to their native justice and magnanimity, and we have conjured them by the ties of our common kindred to disavow these usurpations, which, would inevitably interrupt our connections and correspondence. They too have been deaf to the voice of justice and of consanguinity. We must, therefore, acquiesce in the necessity, which denounces our Separation, and hold them, as we hold the rest of mankind, Enemies in War, in Peace Friends.

We, therefore, the Representatives of the united States of America, in General Congress, Assembled, appealing to the Supreme Judge of the world for the rectitude of our intentions, do, in the Name, and by Authority of the good People of these Colonies, solemnly publish and declare, That these United Colonies are, and of Right ought to be Free and Independent States; that they are Absolved from all Allegiance to the British Crown, and that all political connection between them and the

State of Great Britain, is and ought to be totally dissolved; and that as Free and Independent States, they have full Power to levy War, conclude Peace, contract Alliances, establish Commerce, and to do all other Acts and Things which Independent States may of right do. And for the support of this Declaration, with a firm reliance on the protection of divine Providence, we mutually pledge to each other our Lives, our Fortunes and our sacred Honor.

## The 56 signatures on the Declaration:

**Connecticut:**
Roger Sherman
Samuel Huntington
William Williams
Oliver Wolcott

**Delaware:**
Caesar Rodney
George Read
Thomas McKean

**Georgia:**
Button Gwinnett
Lyman Hall
George Walton

**Maryland:**
Samuel Chase
William Paca
Thomas Stone
Charles Carroll of
Carrollton

**Massachusetts:**
Samuel Adams
John Adams
John Hancock
Robert Treat Paine
Elbridge Gerry

**New Hampshire:**
Josiah Bartlett
William Whipple
Matthew Thornton

**New Jersey:**
Richard Stockton
John Witherspoon
Francis Hopkinson
John Hart
Abraham Clark

**New York:**
William Floyd
Philip Livingston
Francis Lewis
Lewis Morris

**North Carolina:**
William Hooper
Joseph Hewes
John Penn

**South Carolina:**
Edward Rutledge
Thomas Heyward, Jr.
Thomas Lynch, Jr.
Arthur Middleton

**Pennsylvania:**
Robert Morris
Benjamin Rush
Benjamin Franklin
John Morton
George Clymer
James Smith
George Taylor
James Wilson
George Ross

**Rhode Island:**
Stephen Hopkins
William Ellery

**Virginia:**
George Wythe
Richard Henry Lee
Thomas Jefferson
Benjamin Harrison
Thomas Nelson, Jr.
Francis Lightfoot Lee
Carter Braxton

# APPENDIX E:
# THE CONSTITUTION OF THE UNITED STATES OF AMERICA

### Preamble to the Constitution of the United States

We the people of the United States, in order to form a more perfect Union, establish justice, insure domestic tranquility, provide for the common defence, promote the general welfare, and secure the blessings of liberty to ourselves and our posterity, do ordain and establish this Constitution for the United States of America.

### ARTICLE I

**Section 1.** All legislative powers herein granted shall be vested in a Congress of the United States which shall consist of a Senate and House of Representatives.

**Section 2.** The House of Representatives shall be composed of members chosen every second year by the people of the several States, and the electors in each State shall have the qualifications requisite for electors of the most numerous branch of the State legislature.

No person shall be a Representative who shall not have attained to the age of twenty-five years and been seven years a citizen of the United States, and who shall not, when elected, be an inhabitant of that State in which he shall be chosen.

∞ [Representatives and direct taxes shall be apportioned among the several States which may be included within this Union, according to their respective numbers, which shall be determined by adding to the whole number of free persons, including those bound to service for a term of years, and excluding Indians not taxed, three fifths of all other persons.] The actual enumeration shall be made within three years after the first meeting of the Congress of the United States, and within every subsequent term of ten years, in such manner as they shall by law direct. The number of Representatives shall not exceed one for every thirty thousand but each State shall have at least one Representative; and until such enumeration shall be made, the State of New Hampshire shall be entitled to choose three, Massachusetts eight, Rhode Island and Providence Plantations one, Connecticut five, New York six; New Jersey four, Pennsylvania eight,

Delaware one, Maryland six, Virginia ten, North Carolina five, South Carolina five, and Georgia three.

∞ (The preceding portion in brackets is amended by the Fourteenth Amendment, Section 2).

When vacancies happen in the representation from any State, the executive authority thereof shall issue writs of election to fill such vacancies.

The House of Representatives shall choose their Speaker and other officers; and shall have the sole power of impeachment.

**Section 3.** The Senate of the United States shall be composed of two Senators from each State, chosen by the legislature thereof, for six years; and each Senator shall have one vote.

Immediately after they shall be assembled in consequence of the first election, they shall be divided as equally as may be into three classes. The seats of the Senators of the first class shall be vacated at the expiration of the second year, of the second class at the expiration of the fourth year, and of the third class at the expiration of the sixth year, so that one-third may be chosen every second year; and if vacancies happen by resignation, or otherwise, during the recess of the legislature of any State, the Executive thereof may make temporary appointments until the next meeting of the legislature, which shall then fill such vacancies.

No person shall be a Senator who shall not have attained to the age of thirty years and been nine years a citizen of the United States, and who shall not, when elected, be an inhabitant of that State for which he shall be chosen.

The Vice-President of the United States shall be President of the Senate but shall have no vote unless they be equally divided.

The Senate shall choose their other officers, and also a President pro tempore, in the absence of the Vice-President, or when he shall exercise the office of President of the United States.

The Senate shall have the sole power to try all impeachments. When sitting for that purpose, they shall be on oath or affirmation. When the President of the United States is tried, the Chief Justice shall preside: and no person shall be convicted without the concurrence of two thirds of the members present.

Judgment in cases of impeachment shall not extend further than to removal from office and disqualification to hold and enjoy any office of honor, trust, or profit under the United States: but the party convicted shall nevertheless be liable and subject to indictment, trial, judgment and punishment according to Law.

**Section 4.** The times, places, and manner of holding elections for Senators and Representatives shall be prescribed in each State by the legislature thereof; but the Congress may at any time by law make or alter such regulations except as to the places of choosing Senators.

The Congress shall assemble at least once in every year, and such meeting shall be on the first Monday in December, unless they shall by law appoint a different day.

**Section 5.** Each House shall be the judge of the elections, returns, and qualifications of its own members, and a majority of each shall constitute a quorum to do business; but a smaller number may adjourn from day to day and may be authorized to compel the attendance of absent members, in such manner, and under such penalties as each House may provide.

Each House may determine the rules of its proceedings, punish its members for disorderly behavior, and, with the concurrence of two thirds, expel a member.

Each House shall keep a journal of its proceedings and from time to time publish the same, excepting such parts as may in their judgment require secrecy; and the yeas and nays of the members of either House on any question shall, at the desire of one fifth of those present, be entered on the Journal.

Neither House, during the session of Congress, shall, without the consent of the other, adjourn for more than three days nor to any other place than that in which the two Houses shall be sitting.

**Section 6.** The Senators and Representatives shall receive a compensation for their services, to be ascertained by law, and paid out of the Treasury of the United States. They shall in all cases except treason, felony, and breach of the peace, be privileged from arrest during their attendance at the session of their respective Houses and in going to and returning from the same; and for any speech or debate in either House they shall not be questioned in any other place.

No Senator or Representative shall, during the time for which he was elected, be appointed to any civil office under the authority of the United States which shall have been created or the emoluments whereof shall have been increased during such time; and no person holding any office under the United States shall be a member of either House during his continuance in office.

**Section 7.** All bills for raising revenue shall originate in the House of Representatives; but the Senate may propose or concur with amendments as on other bills.

Every bill which shall have passed the House of Representatives and the Senate shall, before it becomes a law, be presented to the President of the United States; if he approve, he shall sign it, but if not he shall return it, with his objections, to that House in which it shall have originated, who shall enter the objections at large on their journal and proceed to reconsider it. If, after such reconsideration, two thirds of that House shall agree to pass the bill, it shall be sent, together with the objections, to the other House, by which it shall likewise be reconsidered, and if approved by two thirds of that House, it shall become a law. But in all such cases, the votes of both Houses shall be determined by yeas and nays and the names of the persons voting for and against the bill shall be entered on the journal of each House respectively. If any bill shall not be returned by the President within ten days (Sundays excepted) after it shall have been presented to him, the same shall be a law in like manner as if he had signed it unless the Congress, by their adjournment, prevent its return, in which case it shall not be a law.

Every order, resolution, or vote to which the concurrence of the Senate and House of Representatives may be necessary (except on a question of adjournment) shall be presented to the President of the United States; and before the same shall take effect shall be approved by him, or, being disapproved by him, shall be repassed by two thirds of the Senate and House of Representatives according to the rules and limitations prescribed in the case of a bill.

**Section 8.** The Congress shall have power to lay and collect taxes, duties, imposts, and excises to pay the debts and provide for the common defense and general welfare of the United States; but all duties, imposts, and excises shall be uniform throughout the United States;

To borrow money on the credit of the United States;

To regulate commerce with foreign nations and among the several States and with the Indian tribes;

To establish an uniform rule of naturalization and uniform laws on the subject of bankruptcies throughout the United States;

To coin money, regulate the value thereof and of foreign coin, and fix the standard of weights and measures;

To provide for the punishment of counterfeiting the securities and current coin of the United States;

To establish post offices and post roads;

To promote the progress of science and useful arts by securing for limited times to authors and inventors the exclusive rights to their respective writings and discoveries;

To constitute tribunals inferior to the Supreme Court;

To define and punish piracies and felonies committed on the high seas and offences against the law of nations;

To declare war, grant letters of marque and reprisal, and make rules concerning captures on land and water;

To raise and support armies, but no appropriation of money to that use shall be for a longer term than two years;

To provide and maintain a Navy;

To make rules for the government and regulation of the land and naval forces;

To provide for calling forth the militia to execute the laws of the Union, suppress insurrections, and repel invasions;

To provide for organizing, arming, and disciplining the militia and for governing such part of them as may be employed in the service of the United States, reserving to the States respectively the appointment of the officers and the authority of training the militia according to the discipline prescribed by Congress;

To exercise exclusive legislation in all cases whatsoever over such district (not exceeding ten miles square) as may, by cession of particular States and the acceptance of Congress, become the seat of the government of the United States, and to exercise like authority over all places purchased by the consent of the legislature of the State in which the same shall be for the erection of forts, magazines, arsenals, dockyards, and other needful buildings;—and

To make all laws which shall be necessary and proper for carrying into execution the foregoing powers and all other powers vested by this Constitution in the government of the United States or in any department or officer thereof.

**Section 9.** The migration or importation of such persons as any of the States now existing shall think proper to admit shall not be prohibited by the Congress prior to the year one thousand eight hundred and eight, but a tax or duty may be imposed on such importation not exceeding ten dollars for each person.

The privilege of the writ of Habeas Corpus shall not be suspended unless when in cases of rebellion or invasion the public safety may require it.

No bill of attainder or ex post facto law shall be passed.

No capitation or other direct tax shall be laid unless in proportion to the census or enumeration herein before directed to be taken.

No tax or duty shall be laid on articles exported from any State.

No preference shall be given by any regulation of commerce or revenue to the ports of one State over those of another: nor shall vessels bound to or from one State be obliged to enter, clear, or pay duties in another.

No money shall be drawn from the Treasury but in consequence of appropriations made by law; and a regular statement and account of the receipts and expenditures of all public money shall be published from time to time.

No title of nobility shall be granted by the United States: and no person holding any office of profit or trust under them shall, without the consent of the Congress, accept of any present, emolument, office, or title of any kind whatever from any king, prince, or foreign State.

**Section 10.** No State shall enter into any treaty, alliance, or confederation; grant letters of marque and reprisal; coin money, emit bills of credit; make any thing but gold and silver coin a tender in payment of debts; pass any bill of attainder, ex post facto law, or law impairing the obligation of contracts, or grant any title of nobility.

No State shall, without the consent of the Congress, lay any imposts of duties on imports or exports except what may be absolutely necessary for executing its inspection laws: and the net produce of all duties and imposts laid by any State on imports or exports shall be for the use of the Treasury of the United States; and all such laws shall be subject to the revision and control of the Congress.

No State shall, without the consent of Congress, lay any duty of tonnage, keep troops, or ships of war in time of peace, enter into any agreement or compact with another State or with a foreign power, or engage in war, unless actually invaded, or in such imminent danger as will not admit of delay.

## ARTICLE II

**Section 1.** The executive power shall be vested in a President of the United States of America. He shall hold his office during the term of four years and, together with the Vice-President chosen for the same term, be elected as follows:

Each State shall appoint, in such manner as the legislature thereof may direct, a number of electors equal to the whole number of Senators and Representatives to which the State may be entitled in the Congress: but no Senator or Representative or person holding an office of trust or profit under the United States shall be appointed an elector.

∞ ["The electors shall meet in their respective States and vote by ballot for two persons of whom one at least shall not be an inhabitant of the same State with themselves. And they shall make a list of all the persons voted for and of the number of votes for each; which list they shall sign and certify and transmit sealed to the seat of the government of the United States, directed to the President of the Senate. The President of the Senate shall, in the presence of the Senate and House of Representatives, open all the certificates and the votes shall then be counted. The person having the greatest number of votes shall be the President if such number be a majority of the whole number of electors appointed; and if there be more than one who have such majority and have an equal number of votes, then the House of Representatives shall immediately choose by ballot one of them for President; and if no person have a majority, then from the five highest on the list the said House shall in like manner choose the President. But in choosing the President, the votes shall be taken by States, the representation from each State having one vote; a quorum for this purpose shall consist of a member or members from two-thirds of the States, and a majority of all the States shall be necessary to a choice. In every case, after the choice of the President, the person having the greatest number of votes of the electors shall be the Vice-President. But if there should remain two or more who have equal votes, the Senate shall choose from them by ballot the Vice-President."]

∞ (The preceding section has been superseded by the Twelfth Amendment).

The Congress may determine the time of choosing the electors and the day on which they shall give their votes; which day shall be the same throughout the United States.

No person except a natural born citizen, or a citizen of the United States at the time of the adoption of this Constitution, shall be eligible to the office of President; neither shall any person be eligible to that office who shall not have attained to the age of thirty-five years and been fourteen years a resident within the United States.

In case of the removal of the President from office, or of his death, resignation, or inability to discharge the powers and duties of the said office, the same shall devolve on the Vice-President, and the Congress may by law provide for the case of removal, death, resignation, or inability, both of the President and Vice-President, declaring what officer shall then act as President, and such officer shall act accordingly until the disability be removed or a President shall be elected.

The President shall, at stated times, receive for his services a compensation which shall neither be increased nor diminished during the period for which he shall have been elected, and he shall not receive within that period any other emolument from the United States or any of them.

Before he enter on the execution of his office, he shall take the following oath or affirmation: — "I do solemnly swear (or affirm) that I will faithfully execute the office of President of the United States and will, to the best of my ability, preserve, protect, and defend the Constitution of the United States."

**Section 2.** The President shall be Commander in Chief of the Army and Navy of the United States, and of the militia of the several States when called into the actual service of the United States; he may require the opinion, in writing, of the principal officer in each of the executive departments upon any subject relating to the duties of their respective offices, and he shall have power to grant reprieves and pardons for offenses against the United States, except in cases of impeachment.

He shall have power, by and with the advice and consent of the Senate, to make treaties, provided two thirds of the Senators present concur; and he shall nominate, and by and with the advice and consent of the Senate, shall appoint Ambassadors, other public Ministers and Consuls, Judges of the Supreme Court, and all other Officers of the United States, whose appointments are not herein otherwise provided for and which shall be established by law: but the Congress may by law vest the appointment of such inferior officers as they think proper in the President alone, in the Courts of law, or in the heads of departments.

The President shall have power to fill up all vacancies that may happen during the recess of the Senate by granting commissions which shall expire at the end of their next session.

**Section 3.** He shall from time to time give to the Congress information of the state of the Union and recommend to their consideration such measures as he shall judge necessary and expedient; he may, on extraordinary occasions, convene both Houses, or either of them, and in case of disagreement between them with respect to the time of adjournment, he may adjourn them to such time as he shall think proper; he shall receive Ambassadors and other public Ministers; he shall take care that the laws be faithfully executed, and shall commission all the officers of the United States.

**Section 4.** The President, Vice-President, and all civil officers of the United States shall be removed from office on impeachment for and conviction of treason, bribery, or other high crimes and misdemeanors.

## ARTICLE III

**Section 1.** The judicial power of the United States shall be vested in one Supreme Court and in such inferior Courts as the Congress may from time to time ordain and establish. The Judges, both of the Supreme and inferior Courts, shall hold their offices during good behavior and shall, at stated times, receive for their services a compensation which shall not be diminished during their continuance in office.

**Section 2.** The judicial power shall extend to all cases in law and equity arising under this Constitution, the laws of the United States, and treaties made, or which shall be made, under their authority:—to all cases affecting Ambassadors, other public Ministers and Consuls;—to all cases of admiralty and maritime jurisdiction;—to controversies to which the United States shall be a party;— to controversies between two or more States;—between a State and citizens of another State;—between citizens of different States,—between citizens of the same State claiming lands under grants of different States, and between a State, or the citizens thereof, and foreign States, citizens, or subjects.

In all cases affecting Ambassadors, other public Ministers and Consuls, and those in which a State shall be party, the Supreme Court shall have original jurisdiction. In all the other cases before mentioned, the Supreme Court shall have appellate jurisdiction both as to law and fact with such exceptions and under such regulations as the Congress shall make.

The trial of all crimes, except in cases of impeachment, shall be by jury; and such trial shall be held in the State where the said crimes shall have been committed; but when not committed within any State, the trial shall be at such place or places as the Congress may by law have directed.

**Section 3.** Treason against the United States shall consist only in levying war against them or in adhering to their enemies, giving them aid and comfort. No person shall be convicted of treason unless on the testimony of two witnesses to the same overt act or on confession in open court.

The Congress shall have power to declare the punishment of treason, but no attainder of treason shall work corruption of blood or forfeiture except during the life of the person attainted.

### ARTICLE IV

**Section 1.** Full faith and credit shall be given in each State to the public acts, records, and judicial proceedings of every other State. And the Congress may by general laws prescribe the manner in which such acts, records, and proceedings shall be proved, and the effect thereof.

**Section 2.** The citizens of each State shall be entitled to all privileges and immunities of citizens in the several States.

A person charged in any State with treason, felony, or other crime, who shall flee from justice and be found in another State, shall on demand of the executive authority of the State from which he fled, be delivered up to be removed to the State having jurisdiction of the crime.

No person held to service or labor in one State under the laws thereof, escaping into another, shall, in consequence of any law or regulation therein, be discharged from such service or labor, but shall be delivered up on claim of the party to whom such service or labor may be due.

**Section 3.** New States may be admitted by the Congress into this Union; but no new State shall be formed or erected within the jurisdiction of any other State; nor any State be formed by the junction of two or more States or parts of States without the consent of the legislatures of the States concerned as well as of the Congress.

The Congress shall have power to dispose of and make all needful rules and regulations respecting the territory or other property belonging to the United States; and nothing in this Constitution shall be so construed as to prejudice any claims of the United States or of any particular State.

**Section 4.** The United States shall guarantee to every State in this Union a republican form of government and shall protect each of them against invasion; and on application of the legislature, or of the Executive (when the legislature cannot be convened), against domestic violence.

## ARTICLE V

The Congress, whenever two thirds of both Houses shall deem it necessary, shall propose amendments to this Constitution or, on the application of the legislatures of two thirds of the several States, shall call a convention for proposing amendments which, in either case, shall be valid to all intents and purposes as part of this Constitution when ratified by the legislatures of three fourths of the several States or by conventions in three fourths thereof as the one or the other mode of ratification may be proposed by the Congress; provided that no amendment which may be made prior to the year one thousand eight hundred and eight shall in any manner affect the first and fourth clauses in the ninth section of the first article; and that no State, without its consent, shall be deprived of its equal suffrage in the Senate.

## ARTICLE VI

All debts contracted and engagements entered into before the adoption of this Constitution shall be as valid against the United States under this Constitution as under the Confederation.

This Constitution and the laws of the United States which shall be made in pursuance thereof; and all treaties made or which shall be made, under the authority of the United States shall be the supreme law of the land; and the judges in every State shall be bound thereby, anything in the Constitution or laws of any State to the contrary notwithstanding.

The Senators and Representatives before mentioned, and the members of the several State legislatures, and all executive and judicial officers both of the United States and of the several States, shall be bound by oath or affirmation to support this Constitution; but no religious test shall ever be required as a qualification to any office or public trust under the United States.

## ARTICLE VII

The ratification of the conventions of nine States shall be sufficient for the establishment of this Constitution between the States so ratifying the same.

DONE in convention by the unanimous consent of the States present the seventeenth day of September in the Year of our Lord one thousand seven hundred and eighty seven, and of the independence of the United States of America the twelfth.

## Amendments to the Constitution

### AMENDMENT I
(First ten amendments adopted June 15, 1790)

Congress shall make no law respecting an establishment of religion or prohibiting the free exercise thereof; or abridging the freedom of speech, or of the press; or the right of the people peaceably to assemble and to petition the government for a redress of grievances.

### AMENDMENT II
A well regulated militia being necessary to the security of a free State, the right of the people to keep and bear arms shall not be infringed.

### AMENDMENT III
No soldier shall in time of peace be quartered in any house without the consent of the owner, nor in time of war but in a manner to be prescribed by law.

### AMENDMENT IV
The right of the people to be secure in their persons, houses, papers, and effects, against unreasonable searches and seizures shall not be violated, and no warrants shall issue but upon probable cause supported by oath or affirmation, and particularly describing the place to be searched and the persons or things to be seized.

### AMENDMENT V
No person shall be held to answer for a capital or otherwise infamous crime unless on a presentment or indictment of a grand jury, except in cases arising in the land or naval forces or in the militia when in actual service in time of war or public danger; nor shall any person be subject for the same offence to be twice put in jeopardy of life or limb; nor shall be compelled in any criminal case to be a witness against himself, nor be deprived of life, liberty, or property, without due process of law; nor shall private property be taken for public use without just compensation.

## AMENDMENT VI

In all criminal prosecutions, the accused shall enjoy the right to a speedy and public trial by an impartial jury of the State and district wherein the crime shall have been committed, which district shall have been previously ascertained by law, and to be informed of the nature and cause of the accusation; to be confronted with the witnesses against him; to have compulsory process for obtaining witnesses in his favor, and to have the assistance of counsel for his defence.

## AMENDMENT VII

In suits at common law, where the value in controversy shall exceed twenty dollars, the right of trial by jury shall be preserved, and no fact tried by a jury shall be otherwise reexamined in any Court of the United States than according to the rules of the common law.

## AMENDMENT VIII

Excessive bail shall not be required nor excessive fines imposed, nor cruel and unusual punishments inflicted.

## AMENDMENT IX

The enumeration in the Constitution of certain rights shall not be construed to deny or disparage others retained by the people.

## AMENDMENT X

The powers not delegated to the United States by the Constitution nor prohibited by it to the States are reserved to the States respectively or to the people.

## AMENDMENT XI

(Adopted January 8, 1798)

The judicial power of the United States shall not be construed to extend to any suit in law or equity commenced or prosecuted against one of the United States by citizens of another State or by citizens or subjects of any foreign State.

## AMENDMENT XII

(Adopted September 25, 1804)

The electors shall meet in their respective States and vote by ballot for President and Vice-President, one of whom, at least, shall not be an inhabitant of the same State with themselves; they shall name in their ballots the person voted for as President and in distinct ballots the person voted for as Vice-President, and they shall make distinct lists of all persons voted for as President and of all persons voted for as Vice-President, and of the number of votes for each, which lists they shall sign and certify and transmit sealed to the seat of the government of the United States, directed to the President of the Senate;—the President of the Senate shall, in the presence of the Senate and House of Representatives, open all the certificates and the votes shall then be counted;—the person having the greatest number of votes for President shall be the President if such number be a majority of the whole number of electors appointed; and if no person have such majority, then from the persons having the highest numbers not exceeding three on the list of those voted for as President, the House of Representatives shall choose immediately by ballot the President. But in choosing the President, the votes shall be taken by States, the representation from each State having one vote; a quorum for this purpose shall consist of a member or members from two-thirds of the States and a majority of all the States shall be necessary to a choice. And if the House of Representatives shall not choose a President whenever the right of choice shall devolve upon them, before the fourth day of March next following, then the Vice-President shall act as President, as in the case of the death or other constitutional disability of the President. The person having the greatest number of votes as Vice-President shall be the Vice-President if such number be a majority of the whole number of electors appointed, and if no person have a majority, then from the two highest numbers on the list the Senate shall choose the Vice-President; a quorum for the purpose shall consist of two-thirds of the whole number of Senators and a majority of the whole number shall be necessary to a choice. But no person constitutionally ineligible to the office of President shall be eligible to that of Vice-President of the United States.

## AMENDMENT XIII
(Adopted December 18, 1865)

**Section 1.** Neither slavery nor involuntary servitude, except as a punishment for crime whereof the party shall have been duly convicted, shall exist within the United States or any place subject to their jurisdiction.

**Section 2.** Congress shall have power to enforce this article by appropriate legislation.

## AMENDMENT XIV
(Adopted July 21, 1868)

**Section 1.** All persons born or naturalized in the United States and subject to the jurisdiction thereof are citizens of the United States and of the State wherein they reside. No State shall make or enforce any law which shall abridge the privileges or immunities of citizens of the United States; nor shall any State deprive any person of life, liberty, or property, without due process of law; nor deny to any person within its jurisdiction the equal protection of the laws.

**Section 2.** Representatives shall be apportioned among the several States according to their respective numbers, counting the whole number of persons in each State, excluding Indians not taxed. But when the right to vote at any election for the choice of electors for President and Vice-President of the United States, Representatives in Congress, the Executive and Judicial officers of a State, or the members of the Legislature thereof, is denied to any of the male inhabitants of each State, being twenty-one years of age and citizens of the United States, or in any way abridged, except for participation in rebellion or other crime, the basis of representation therein shall be reduced in the proportion which the number of such male citizens shall bear to the whole number of male citizens twenty-one years of age in such State.

**Section 3.** No person shall be a Senator or Representative in Congress or elector of President and Vice-President, or hold any office, civil or military, under the United States or under any State who, having previously taken an oath as a member of Congress or as an officer of the United States or as a member of any State legislature or as an executive or judicial officer of any State, to support the Constitution of the United States, shall have engaged in insurrection or rebellion against the same or given aid or comfort to the enemies thereof. But Congress may by a vote of two-thirds of each House remove such disability.

**Section 4.** The validity of the public debt of the United States, authorized by law, including debts incurred for payment of pensions and bounties for services in suppressing insurrection or rebellion, shall not be questioned.

But neither the United States nor any State shall assume or pay any debt or obligation incurred in aid of insurrection or rebellion against the United States or any claim for the loss or emancipation of any slave; but all such debts, obligations, and claims shall be held illegal and void.

**Section 5.** The Congress shall have power to enforce by appropriate legislation the provisions of this article.

## AMENDMENT XV
(Adopted March 30, 1870)

**Section 1.** The right of citizens of the United States to vote shall not be denied or abridged by the United States or by any State on account of race, color, or previous condition of servitude.

**Section 2.** The Congress shall have power to enforce this article by appropriate legislation.

## AMENDMENT XVI
(Adopted February 25, 1913)

The Congress shall have power to lay and collect taxes on incomes, from whatever source derived, without apportionment among the several States and without regard to any census or enumeration.

## AMENDMENT XVII
(Adopted May 31, 1913)

The Senate of the United States shall be composed of two Senators from each State, elected by the people thereof for six years; and each Senator shall have one vote. The electors in each State shall have the qualifications requisite for electors of the most numerous branch of the State legislatures.

When vacancies happen in the representation of any State in the Senate, the executive authority of such State shall issue writs of election to fill such vacancies; Provided that the legislature of any State may empower the executive thereof to make temporary appointments until the people fill the vacancies by election as the legislature may direct.

This amendment shall not be so construed as to affect the election or term of any Senator chosen before it becomes valid as a part of the Constitution.

## AMENDMENT XVIII
(Adopted January 29, 1919)

**Section 1.** After one year from the ratification of this article the manufacture, sale, or transportation of intoxicating liquors within, the importation thereof into, or the exportation thereof from the United States and all territory subject to the jurisdiction thereof for beverage purposes is hereby prohibited.

**Section 2.** The Congress and the several States shall have concurrent power to enforce this article by appropriate legislation.

**Section 3.** This article shall be inoperative unless it shall have been ratified as an amendment to the Constitution by the legislatures of the several States, as provided in the Constitution, within seven years from the date of the submission hereof to the States by the Congress.

## AMENDMENT XIX
(Adopted August 26, 1920)

The right of citizens of the United States to vote shall not be denied or abridged by the United States or by any State on account of sex.

Congress shall have power to enforce this article by appropriate legislation.

## AMENDMENT XX
(Adopted January 23, 1933)

**Section 1.** The terms of the President and Vice-President shall end at noon on the 20th day of January, and the terms of Senators and Representatives at noon on the 3rd day of January, of the years in which such terms would have ended if this article had not been ratified; and the terms of their successors shall then begin.

**Section 2.** The Congress shall assemble at least once in every year and such meeting shall begin at noon on the 3rd day of January unless they shall by law appoint a different day.

**Section 3.** If, at the time fixed for the beginning of the term of the President, the President elect shall have died, the Vice-President elect shall become President. If a President shall not have been chosen before the time fixed for the beginning of his term, or if the President elect shall have failed to qualify, then the Vice-President elect shall act as President until a President shall have qualified; and the Congress may by law provide for the case wherein neither a President elect nor a Vice-President elect shall have qualified, declaring who shall then act as President, or the manner in which one who is to act shall be selected, and such person shall act accordingly until a President or Vice-President shall have qualified.

**Section 4.** The Congress may by law provide for the case of the death of any of the persons from whom the House of Representatives may choose a President whenever the right of choice shall have devolved upon them, and for the case of the death of any of the persons from whom the

Senate may choose a Vice-President whenever the right of choice shall have devolved upon them.

**Section 5.** Sections 1 and 2 shall take effect on the 15th day of October following the ratification of this article (Oct. 1933).

**Section 6.** This article shall be inoperative unless it shall have been ratified as an amendment to the Constitution by the Legislatures of three-fourths of the several States within seven years from the date of its submission.

## AMENDMENT XXI
(Adopted December 5, 1933)

**Section 1.** The eighteenth article of amendment to the Constitution of the United States is hereby repealed.

**Section 2.** The transportation or importation into any State, territory, or possession of the United States for delivery or use therein of intoxicating liquors, in violation of the laws thereof, is hereby prohibited.

**Section 3.** This article shall be inoperative unless it shall have been ratified as an amendment to the Constitution by conventions in the several States, as provided in the Constitution, within seven years from the date of the submission hereof to the States by the Congress.

## AMENDMENT XXII
(Adopted February 27, 1951)

**Section 1.** No person shall be elected to the office of the President more than twice, and no person who has held the office of President, or acted as President, for more than two years of a term to which some other person was elected President shall be elected to the office of the President more than once. But this Article shall not apply to any person holding the office of President when this Article was proposed by the Congress, and shall not prevent any person who may be holding the office of President, or acting as President, during the term within which this Article becomes operative from holding the office of President or acting as President during the remainder of such term.

**Section 2.** This article shall be inoperative unless it shall have been ratified as an amendment to the Constitution by the Legislatures of three-fourths of the several States within seven years from the date of its submission to the States by the Congress.

## AMENDMENT XXIII
(Adopted March 29, 1961)

**Section 1.** The District constituting the seat of government of the United States shall appoint in such manner as the Congress may direct:

A number of electors of President and Vice-President equal to the whole number of Senators and Representatives in Congress to which the District would be entitled if it were a State, but in no event more than the least populous State; they shall be in addition to those appointed by the States, but they shall be considered, for the purposes of the election of President and Vice-President, to be electors appointed by a State; and they shall meet in the District and perform such duties as provided by the twelfth article of amendment.

**Section 2.** The Congress shall have power to enforce this article by appropriate legislation.

## AMENDMENT XXIV
(Adopted January 23, 1964)

**Section 1.** The right of citizens of the United States to vote in any primary or other election for President or Vice-President, for electors for President or Vice-President, or for Senator or Representative in Congress, shall not be denied or abridged by the United States or any State by reason of failure to pay any poll tax or other tax.

**Section 2.** The Congress shall have power to enforce this article by appropriate legislation.

## AMENDMENT XXV
(Adopted February 10, 1965)

**Section 1.** In case of the removal of the President from office or of his death or resignation, the Vice-President shall become President.

**Section 2.** Whenever there is a vacancy in the office of the Vice-President, the President shall nominate a Vice-President who shall take office upon confirmation by a majority vote of both houses of Congress.

**Section 3.** Whenever the President transmits to the President pro tempore of the Senate and the Speaker of the House of Representatives his written declaration that he is unable to discharge the powers and duties of his office, and until he transmits to them a written declaration to the contrary, such powers and duties shall be discharged by the Vice-President as acting President.

**Section 4.** Whenever the Vice-President and a majority of either the principal officers of the executive departments or of such other body as Congress may by law provide, transmit to the President pro tempore of the Senate and the Speaker of the House of Representatives their written declaration that the President is unable to discharge the powers and duties of his office, the Vice-President shall immediately assume the powers and duties of the office as acting President

Thereafter, when the President transmits to the President pro tempore of the Senate and the Speaker of the House of Representatives his written declaration that no inability exists, he shall resume the powers and duties of his office unless the Vice-President and a majority of either the principal officers of the executive department or of such other body as Congress may by law provide, transmit within four days to the President pro tempore of the Senate and the Speaker of the House of Representatives their written declaration that the President is unable to discharge the powers and duties of his office. Thereupon Congress shall decide the issue, assembling within forty-eight hours for that purpose if not in session. If the Congress, within twenty-one days after receipt of the latter written declaration, or, if Congress is not in session, within twenty-one days after Congress is required to assemble, determines by two-thirds vote of both houses that the President is unable to discharge the powers and duties of his office, the Vice-President shall continue to discharge the same as acting President; otherwise, the President shall resume the powers and duties of his office.

### AMENDMENT XXVI
(Adopted July 1, 1971)

**Section 1.** The right of citizens of the United States, who are 18 years of age or older, to vote shall not be denied or abridged by the United States or any state on account of age.

**Section 2.** The Congress shall have the power to enforce this article by appropriate legislation.

### AMENDMENT XXVII
(Adopted May 7, 1992)

No law varying the compensation for the services of the Senators and Representatives shall take effect until an election of Representatives shall have intervened.

# APPENDIX F:
# ENDNOTES

[1] The Declaration of Independence, para. 2 (U.S. 1776).

[2] Thomas Jefferson, *The Jeffersonian Cyclopedia* (Funk & Wagnalls company, 1900), page 326

[3] David Barton, *Original Intent: The Courts, the Constitution, and Religion* (WallBuilder Press, 2005), page 215

[4] *Stone* v. *Graham,* 449 U.S. 39, 42 (1980).

[5] Benjamin Rush, *Essays, Literary, Moral and Philosophical* (Philadelphia: Thomas and Samuel Bradford, 1798), p. 112, "Defense of the Use of the Bible as a School Book."

[6] *Santa Fe* v. *Doe,* 530 U.S. 290 (2000).

[7] The Declaration of Independence, para. 2 (U.S. 1776).

[8] Newdow, 292 F. 3d 597, 607 (9th Cir. 2002), *amended by* 328 F. 3d 466, (9th Cir. 2003), *rev'd for lack of standing, rev'd sub nom.*, Elk Grove Unified School District v. Newdow, __ U.S. __, 124 S. Ct. 2301 (2004).

[9] U.S. constitution. Art. V

[10] The Declaration of Independence, para. 2 (U.S. 1776).

[11] *Kelo* V. *New London* (04-108) 545 U.S. 469 (2005) 268 Conn. 1, 843 A. 2d 500, affirmed.

[12] William Jay, *The Life of John Jay : With Selections F rom His Correspondence and MiscellaneousP apers* (New York: J. & J. Harper, 1833), Vol. I, pp. 457-458, to the Committee of the Corportaion of the City of New York on June 29, 1826.

[13] I use the words "attributed to" because despite the fact many presidents have credited de Tocqueville for this quote, these exact words did not appear in any of his writings, though he published many very similar statements and was quoted by others as saying these words.

[14] Isaac Krammic & R. Laurence Moore, *The Godless Constitution: The Case Against Religious Correctness* (W. W. Horton, 1996).

[15] 685 A.2d 96 (1991).

[16] 530 U.S. 290 (2000).

[17] 168 F.3d 806 (5th Cir. 1999).

[18] *Valedictorian's faith.*( Brittany McComb); Publication: The New American, 07-AUG-06; Author: Mass, Warren

[19] *BRAVE NEW SCHOOLS, Valedictorian sues over Gospel speech, Diploma withheld until she apologized for declaring Christian faith*; August 30, 2007; WorldNetDaily.com

[20] Letter from John Adams to Thomas Jefferson (June 28, 1813), *in* 2 The Adams-Jefferson Letters, 339-40 (Lester J. Capon ed., University of North Carolina Press, 1959).

[21] Newdow, 292 F. 3d 597 (9th Cir. 2002), *amended by* 328 F. 3d 466 (9th Cir. 2003), *rev'd for lack of standing, rev'd sub.nom.* Elk Grove Unified School District v. Newdow, __ U.S. __, 124 S. Ct. 2301 (2004).

[22] President Woodrow Wilson, Remarks Upon Arrival at Andrews Air Force Base (November 22, 1963) *in* Robert Flood, The Rebirth of America, 12 (The Arthur S. DeMoss Foundation, 1986).

[23] Reverend Nathaniel Randolph Snowden, *Diary and Remembrances*, (Original Manuscript at the Historical Society of Pennsylvania; Call no. PHi.Am.1561-1568).

[24] Jared Sparks, *The Life of Gouverneur Morris*, p. 483 (Boston: Gray and Bowen, 1832).

[25] James Wilson, *Of the General Principles of Law and Obligation*, in The Works of the Honorable James Wilson, pp. 103-105 (Bird Wilson ed., Philadelphia: Lorenzo Press 1804).

[26] 505 U.S. 577 (1992).

[27] William Samuel Johnson, *Commencement Speech to Graduating Class of Columbia University* (1787), *in* John Irving, A Discourse of the Advantages of Classical Learning 141-43 (New York: G. & C. & H. Carvill, 1830).

[28] *Acts* 17:28.

[29] Silas Deane, *The Deane Papers: Collections of the New York Historical Society for the Year 1886* (New York: Printed for the Society, 1887), Vol. I, p. 20, Wednesday, September 7, 1774; see also *Letters of Delegates*, Vol. I, p. 35.

[30] Letter from John Adams to Abigail Adams (Sep. 16,1774), <http://www.masshist.org/digitaladams/aea/cfm/doc.cfm?id=L17740916ja>

[31] James Madison, *Notes of Debates in the Federal Convention of 1787*, at 209-10 (reprinted NY: W.W. Norton & Co., 1987) (1787).

[32] Noah Webster, *An American Dictionary of the English Language* (Springfield: George and Charles Merriam, 1849), "Memoir of the Author," p. xxii.

[33] William G. Webster, *A Speller and Definer* (Philadelphia: J. B. Lippincott Company, 1845), inside front cover.

[34] September, 1811 letter written from St. Petersburg by John Quincy Adams to his son. Appears in the following: Doug Phillips, Editor, *The Bible Lessons of John Quincy Adams for His Son* (San Antonio, TX: Vision Forum, Inc, 2000), p. 15.

[35] From an autographed letter in the possession of *WallBuilders* written by Charles Carroll to Charles W. Wharton, Esq., on September 27, 1825, from Doughoragen, Maryland.

[36] James Iredell, *The Papers of James Iredell*, Don Higginbotham, editor (Raleigh: North Carolina Division of Archives and History, 1976), Vol. I, p. 11 from his 1768 essay on religion.

[37] Edwards Beardsley, *Life and Times of William Samuel Johnson* (Boston: Houghton, Mifflin and Company, 1886), p. 184.

[38] Hugh A. Garland, *The Life of John Randolph of Roanoke* (New York: D. Appleton & Company, 1853), Vol. II, p. 104, from Francis Scott Key to John Randolph.

[39] Robert Treat Paine, *The Papers of Robert Treat Paine,* Stephen T. Riley and Edward W. Hanson, editors (Boston: Massachusetts Historical Society, 1992), Vol. I, p. 48, March/April, 1749.

[40] Benjamin Rush, *The Autobiography of Benjamin Rush,* George W. Corner, editor (Princeton: Princeton University Press for the American Philosophical Society, 1948), p. 166.

[41] Barton, pp. 123-146

[42] *Engel v. Vitale*, 370 U.S. 421, 422 (1962).

[43] U.S. Const. Amend. I.

[44] U.S. Const. Art. I, § 5, cl. 3.

[45] Compiled By Friends, *Works of Fisher Ames* 134 (Boston: T. B. Wait & Co., 1809).

[46] Letter to the Danbury Baptist Association (January 1, 1802), *in* Thomas Jefferson, Jefferson Writings 510 (Merril D. Peterson et al. eds., 1984) (1781).

[47] Everson v. Board of Education, 330 U.S. 1 (1947).

[48] Thomas Jefferson, Letter to the Danbury Baptist Association, *in Thomas Jefferson, Jefferson Writings* 510 (Merrill D. Peterson et al. eds., 1984) (1802): *Believing with you that religion is a matter which lies solely between man and his God, that he owes account to none other for faith or his worship, that the legislative powers of government reach actions only, and not opinions, I contemplate with solemn reverence that act of the whole American people which declared that their legislature should "make no law respecting an establishment of religion, or prohibiting the free exercise thereof," thus building a wall of separation between Church and State.*

[49] *Engle v. Vitale*, 370 U.S. 421 (1962).

[50] Letter to Dr. Joseph Priestly (Washington ed., 441). <http://etext.lib.virginia.edu/etcbin/foley-page?id=JCE1686>.

[51] *Id.*

[52] William Parker Cutler and Julia Perkins Cutler, *Life, Journal, and Correspondence of Rev. Manasseh Cutler* (Cincinnati: Colin Robert Clarke & Co., 1888), Vol. II, p. 66, 119, letter to Joseph Torrey, January 4, 1802. Cutler meant that Jefferson attended church on January 3, 1802, for the first time as President. Bishop Claggett's letter of February 18, 1801, already revealed that as Vice-President, Jefferson went to church services in the House.

[53] *The Holy Bible : New International Version.* 1996, c1984 (electronic ed.) (Dt 8:11-14). Grand Rapids: Zondervan.

[54] Joshua 1:9

[55] Benjamin Rush, *Letters of Benjamin Rush,* L. H. Butterfield, editor (New Jersey: American Philosophical Society, 1951), Vol. I, pp. 532-536, to John Adams on February 24, 1790.

[56] Benjamin Franklin, *The Writings of Benjamin Franklin* , Albert Henry Smyth, editor (New York: McMillan Company, 1907) Vol. V, 1767-1772, p. 220, No. 504. Letter to the Committee of Merchants in Philadelphia, July 9, 1769.

[57] John Locke, *An Essay Concerning Human Understanding* (London: George Routledge and Sons, 1894) 187, Questia, 25 Aug. 2008 <http://www.questia.com/PM.qst?a=o&d=5781714>.

[58] Smith, Adam. *An Inquiry into the Nature and Causes of the Wealth of Nations.* London: Methuen and Co., Ltd., ed. Edwin Cannan, 1904. [Online] available from http://www.econlib.org/LIBRARY/Smith/smWN1.html; accessed 15 July 2008;

[59] HumanEvents.com, April 13, 2007, *"Quote Wars: Milton Friedman vs. Hillary Clinton."* http://www.humanevents.com/article.php?id=20237

[60] CNN. *"The Situation Room: Sojourners Presidential Forum."* 4 June 2007.

[61] Clinton, Hillary Rodham. *It Takes a Village: And Other Lessons Our Children Teach Us.*

[62] Fouhy, Beth. *"San Francisco Rolls Out the Red Carpet for the Clintons."* Associated Press. 29 June 2004.

[63] Ronald Reagan - October 27, 1964. *"A Time for Choosing"*

[64] Thomas Jefferson, *The Writings of Thomas Jefferson* Andrew Lipscomb, editor (Thomas Jefferson Memorial Association: Washington, D.C, 1904) Vol. XIV, p. 466, Letter to Mr. Joseph Milligan, April 6, 1816 (A Note communicated to the Editor).

[65] Ronald Reagan - October 27, 1964. *"A Time for Choosing"*

[66] *Id.*

[67] Benjamin Franklin, *The Writings of Benjamin Franklin,* Albert Smyth, editor (New York: The MacMillan Company, 1907), Vol. 8, p. 613, "1364. Information to Those Who Would Remove to America."

[68] Benjamin Franklin, *The Writings of Benjamin Franklin,* Albert Smyth, editor (New York: The Macmillan Company, 1907) Vol. V, p. 86, "Causes of the American Discontents before 1768."

[69] Benjamin Franklin, *The Writings of Benjamin Franklin* , Albert Henry Smyth, editor (New York: McMillan Company, 1907) Vol. V, 1767-1772, p. 220, No. 504. Letter to the Committee of Merchants in Philadelphia, July 9, 1769.

[70] David Josiah Brewer, Edward Archibald Allen, William Schuyler, *The World's Best Orations: From the Earliest Period to the Present Time* Published by F. P. Kaiser, 1899; p. 3946

[71] Hillary Clinton, Speech delivered May 29, 2007, *Economic Policy: Modern Progressive Vision: Shared Prosperity.* http://www.hillaryclinton.com/news/speech/view/?id=1839

[72] Balz, Dan. *"Oil Firms Turn Katrina Into Profits, Clinton Says."* The Washington Post. 3 September 2005 (p. A10).

[73] The Declaration of Independence, para. 12 (U.S. 1776).

[74] Dr. Kenneth McFarland, *"America's Opportunity."* Speech given 1976.

[75] Milton Friedman, Wall Street Journal, *May 18, 1961*

[76] Milton Friedman, WSJ, *Mar. 7, 1996*

[77] 1781 letter from Benjamin Rush to John Adams.

[78] *Id.*

[79] The Declaration of Independence, para. 32 (U.S. 1776).

[80] *The New King James Version*. 1982 (Jn 15:13). Nashville: Thomas Nelson.

[81] Bancroft Copy of Abraham Lincoln's Gettysburg Address given November 19, 1863. Full text can be found at: http://rmc.library.cornell.edu/gettysburg/good_cause/transcript.htm

[82] The Declaration of Independence, para. 2 (U.S. 1776).

[83] *The New King James Version*. 1982 (Jas 2:26). Nashville: Thomas Nelson.

[84] John Hancock, *Boston Massacre Oration* (March 5, 1774), *in* American Voices: Significant Speeches in American History 41-48 (Longman, 1989).

[85] *Proverbs* 29:2.

[86] *Id.*

[87] James A. Garfield, *A Century of Congress*, Atlantic, July 1877, at 49.

[88] *Recount of Fla. ballots favors Bush* by The Associated Press on 11/12/01

[89] William Wirt, *Sketches of the Life and Character of Patrick Henry* (Philadelphia: James Webster, 1818), pp. 121–123.

[90] *The New King James Version*. 1982 (Ex 18:21). Nashville: Thomas Nelson.

[91] Matthias Burnett, *An Election Sermon, Preached at Hartford, on the Day of the Anniversary Election*, May 12, 1803, at 26-27 (Hartford: Hudson & Goodwin, 1803).

[92] *The New King James Version*. 1982 (Mt 6:21). Nashville: Thomas Nelson.

[93] The Atlantic Monthly, March, 2007, *"They won't know what hit them."*

[94] Samuel Adams, *The Life and Public Services of Samuel Adams,* William Wells, editor (Boston: Little, Brown, and Company, 1865) Vol. III, pp. 414-415, *An Oration Delivered at the State-House in Philadelphia, to a Very Numerous Audience, On Thursday the 1st of August 1776* (Philadelphia/ London(Re-print), 1776.

[95] Benjamin Franklin, *The Papers of Benjamin Franklin*< Leonard Labaree, editor (New Haven, Yale University Press, 1963) Vol. 6, p. 242, Pennsylvania Assembly: Reply to the Governor," November 11, 1755.

[96] John Hancock, *Boston Massacre Oration* (March 5, 1774), *in* American Voices: Significant Speeches in American History 41-48 (Longman, 1989).

[97] Madison, Papers (1840), Vol. III, P. 1324, on August 14, 1787, by John Francis Mercer.

[98] 505 U.S. 577 (1992).

[99] Robert Flood, *The Rebirth of America* (Philadelphia: The Arthur S. DeMoss Foundation, 1986), p. 12.

[100] 32 Journals of the Continental Congress 340 (1787).

[101] *Quoted in* David Barton, The Myth of Separation 268 (WallBuilder Press, 1991).

[102] H.B. 1776, 77th Leg., Reg. Sess. (Tex. 2001).

[103] The Declaration of Independence, para. 2 (U.S. 1776).

# PATRIOT *academy*

sponsored by wallbuilders and the torch of freedom foundation
{ raising up a new generation to **LEAD THE CHANGE** }

## CHALLENGE YOUR IDEA OF GOVERNMENT

At Patriot Academy, you don't just learn about government, you live it. This summer, you and your fellow students, ages 16-25, will take over the Texas state government at the Capitol Building in Austin, Texas. You will work together to form a fully functioning mock government, drafting legislation, running committee meetings, debating bills, electing leaders and passing laws.

## CONFRONT THE ISSUES OF TODAY

In a fast-paced, interactive format, elected officials and experts will explain today's most relevant issues. Through media relations training, public speaking workshops and spirited debate, you will learn to articulate what you believe and why. Patriot Academy will equip you to effect change for the issues that matter most to you, whether as a concerned citizen or political candidate.

## CHAMPION THE CAUSE OF FREEDOM

If you want to be a part of a new generation of young leaders poised to change the future of American politics, join us at Patriot Academy. You won't want to miss it!

FOR MORE INFORMATION OR TO APPLY, VISIT US AT
# WWW.PATRIOTACADEMY.COM

To order more of Rick Green's products, go to
**www.rickgreen.com**

### Is America One Nation Under God?
In Rick's most popular presentation, we discover whether or not our nation was founded on biblical principles
**Available on DVD, audio CD, & booklet**

### The Birth of Freedom
Journey back before 1776, when the first seeds of freedom were planted, to learn about the Revolutionary Strategies of the Founding Fathers. You will also hear about America's first War on Radical Islamic Terrorism & how our first 4 presidents won the same fight America now faces
**Available on DVD & audio CD**

### The Guardian of Liberty
Rick defends the "Pursuit of Happiness" through our free competitive enterprise system, and makes the case for choosing only leaders who have faith in the free market
**Available on DVD & audio CD**

### Collection of Historical Presentations
This set includes a DVD & audio CD of Rick's following presentations: Is America One Nation Under God, The Birth of Freedom, The Guardian of Liberty

# ABOUT THE AUTHOR...

Rick Green is a professional speaker with an emphasis on America's Founding Principles. He served as a Texas State Representative, and has spoken across the nation to crowds as large as 20,000. He has shared the stage with such renowned speakers as Zig Ziglar, David Barton,  Peter Lowe, Charles Jarvis, and Alan Keyes. He currently co-hosts the daily radio talk show "WallBuilders Live!" with David Barton. Rick and his wife, Kara, have four children and reside in Dripping Springs, Texas.

Rick and his family are avid baseball fans. One of their goals is to visit every major league baseball park.

They are half way there....

Rick, Kara, & their kids
at Yankee Stadium

## Freedom's Frame

Freedom's Frame is also available as an unabridged audio book, read by the author

www.rickgreen.com